DREAMING BIG IN SMALL PLACES

By Bishop Emmanuel Owusu Ansah

Web: www.bishopansah.org
Email: info@bishopansah.org

First Printing, 2013

Ingene Publications

63 Fernhead Road

Maida Vale, W9

London.

Web: www.ingenepublishers.com

Email: info@ingenepublishers.com

ISBN: 978-1-909524-13-2

DREAMING BIG IN SMALL PLACES

Printed in the United Kingdom

DREAMING
BIG
—— IN ——
SMALL PLACES

CONTENTS

DEDICATION

This book is dedicated to my miracle son Emmanuel Jassby Ansah Jnr, and the children of this generation who have to dream big even in their small places.

ACKNOWLEDGEMENT

Every dream begins in the heart of one man, but it takes the co-operation and involvement of other people to translate the dream into reality. The birth of this insightful book would not have been possible without the contributions and commitment of certain men and women. These people in essence became my 'dream-builders'. Without their availability, this book would have remained an intangible 'dream' rather than becoming a tangible reality as it stands today.

I wish to acknowledge the following for their effort, contribution, service and support at various stages of this project. Firstly I wish to thank the Pastorate Team of Kingdom Life Ministries (K.L.M.) who loyally committed themselves to minister and take up some of my duties in order to release me to concentrate on the completion of this book – a dream which I have carried for many years.

My sincere gratitude goes to Joana Adu, Miriam Ampomah and Justina Amoah who sacrificed many evenings and nights to prepare this manuscript. Much appreciation also goes to Minister Vivien Odeleye for providing her administrative support and editorial expertise to this project.

I am grateful to Yaw F. Tenkorang whose ingenuity and research facilitated the preparation and structuring of this book.

Also my gratitude goes to Bernard K. Arhin for his graphic design expertise brought on board.

Special thanks go to my wife, Olivia and family for bearing much personal sacrifice as they permitted me to take time away in private for days on end as I pushed towards the completion of this book.

My final thanks go to all our beloved K.L.M. Members and Partners, both at home and abroad, whose all round support and prayers have brought me this far.

To God be the Glory for teaching us all how to DREAM BIG IN SMALL PLACES.

INTRODUCTION

On August 28, 1963, history was to be made. The place was the steps of the Lincoln Memorial. The event was the March on Washington for Jobs and Freedom. There were over 250,000 people present. This is when Martin Luther King delivered the much famed and award winning speech "I Have a Dream." Let me share with you the part of the speech that has made the most waves:

"I have a dream that one day this nation (America) will rise up and live out the true meaning of its creed: "We hold these truths to be self-evident, that all men are created equal."

I have a dream that one day on the red hills of Georgia, the sons of former slaves and the sons of former slave owners will be able to sit down together at the table of brotherhood.

I have a dream that one day even the state of Mississippi, a state sweltering with the heat of injustice, sweltering with the heat of oppression, will be transformed into an oasis of freedom and justice.

I have a dream that my four little children will one day live in a nation where they will not be judged by the color of their skin but by the content of their character.

I have a dream today!

I have a dream that one day, down in Alabama, with its vicious racists, with its governor having his lips dripping with the words of "interposition" and "nullification" -- one day right there in Alabama little black boys and black girls will be able to join hands with little white boys and white girls as sisters and brothers.

I have a dream today!

I have a dream that one day every valley shall be exalted, and every hill and mountain shall be made low, the rough places will be made plain, and the crooked places will be made straight; "and the glory of the Lord shall be revealed and all flesh shall see it together."

This is our hope, and this is the faith that I go back to the South with."

These were the dreams of Martin Luther King about half a century ago. It was a dream that is associated with him and which he laid down his life for. It was a dream he influenced millions of people with though that he did not live to see its full realization. It was this dream that set in motion the fall of the walls of segregation in the United States. Have these dreams been realized today? I would say to a large extent yes. Not only are the sons of slaves and sons of slave owners able to sit together at a table of brotherhood, but a son of a slave has become their president – Barack Obama. He did not mention this in his dream half a century ago but it's a reality today. Though there are still pockets of racism in the United States, yet significant strides have been made.

But it all began with a dream. He had this dream long before he gave the "I Have a Dream" speech. Every great achievement in the history of mankind usually began as a dream. Everything you see today was a dream yesterday. The dreams of yesterday are the realities of today. In the same vein, the dreams of today will be the realities of tomorrow. The future lies in dreams. In actuality, dreams are real. They may not be realistic today, but they are real. Most dreams at the time of conception were not realistic but today they are easy-to-do things. They may not be tangible today but they are real. Every dream begins as intangible before it becomes tangible. They may not be visible, but they are real. They may not look possible but they are real. They may be idealistic, but they are real.

The internet was a dream. Man stepping foot on the moon was a dream. Man flying from one continent to another in a few hours was a dream. Being able to talk to your mother from any point on this planet through the mobile phone you hold in your hands was a dream. The kindle through which you read books was a dream. Locating a place thousands of miles away with your laptop through Google maps without having to be a CIA agent was a dream. Dreams are not visible but they are valuable. Dreams produce real things.

CHAPTER 1

DARE TO DREAM

CLOSE YOUR EYES, PICTURE SOMETHING; ENSURE IT STRIKES THE CHORD OF DESTINY.

Dream lofty dreams, and as you dream, so you shall become. Your vision is the promise of what you shall one day be; your ideal is the prophecy of what you shall at last unveil - *James Allen*.

As you desire to be better, and achieve more, even more must you dare to dream. Nothing happens unless a man dreams. When people stop dreaming, souls are not saved, the sick are not healed, the captives are not set free, the weak are not strengthened, inventions are not created, products are not manufactured, services are not offered, businesses are not built, songs are not written, movies are not made, explorations are not made, cures are not found, people do not break away from negative habits and addictions and people die with their destinies unrevealed.

It is a universal fact that the world loses more from your failure to dream than for your failure in achieving the dream.

Dreams have weakened the hands of oppressors and delivered freedom to millions of people. Dreams have ended wars. Dreams have built skyscrapers. Dreams have built great churches. Dreams have fed the poor and resettled them. Dreams have taken man to the Moon and beyond. Dreams have translated Third World nations into First World nations. Dreams have built multinational organizations. Dreams have developed inventions. Through the dreams of one person, our life is being transformed from one level of glory to another. The great painter, Vincent van Gogh wrote that, *"I dream my painting and I paint my dream."*

The only place where dreams are nullified is in the grave. In your next life, your dreams may no longer be necessary or needed. The day you die, you die with those dreams. There are no dreams in the grave so if you have any dreams to nurture into fruition, then dream them today and wake up to work them into reality. When you stop dreaming, you start dying. I do not want you to look back twenty years from now and see that you could have done more but you did not all because you did not dream or wake up to work out your dream. H. Jackson brown said, *"Twenty years from now you will be more disappointed by the things that you didn't do than by the ones you did do. So throw off the bowlines. Sail away from the safe harbor. Catch the trade winds in your sails. Explore, dream, discover."*

The glory that comes with the realization of a man's dream can outlive his life span. The world is currently being ruled by the dreams of dead men. Democracy is a dead man's dream. The internet was someone's dream. The telephone is a dead man's dream – Alexander Bell. The first computing machine was a dead man's dream – Charles Babbage. The iPad is the dream of a dead man – Steve Jobs. You do not have to die before your dreams make impact. You can see your dreams unfold right before your eyes. Wake up, smell the coffee and spur yourself on to work on the dream. The dreams you have today, could be what will rule the next generation.

In fact, God is a dreamer. He speaks through dreams. The Bible is a collection of God's dreams - His desires, expectations and hopes for man. When you make the desires, expectations and hopes of God yours, you are dreaming the dreams of God and the dreams of God will never fail.

When great men dreamt, they were nowhere near the dream. They dreamt without having the resources needed to finance it. They dreamt without the expertise to get it done. They dreamt without the relevant experience to guide their decisions. They dreamt without the human capital they needed. Their dreams were bigger than them and yet they dreamt. Though they were in the small places of life, yet they dreamt and today their small places have turned into big places. They were dreaming big in small places.

Some of them dreamt of prosperity but were living in poverty. Some were dreaming of skyscrapers when they were living on the streets. Some were dreaming of globe-trotting when they were living in places that were off the map. They were living in holes but were dreaming of being on international arenas. They were dreaming of a blessed life when they were living like the cursed on the earth. They were dreaming big in small places.

If you find yourself in a place where your dreams look far bigger than you, this book is for you. If you find yourself in a place where you do not see how your dreams can come true, this book is for you. If you find yourself in a place that is so obscure that you do not see how your dream can emerge from there, this book is for you. I wrote this book for those of you who have big dreams but you look at your past and present and see that there is a wide gap between the two and so you feel like giving up on the future.

Know this, that every successful person dreamt when he was a 'nobody' and had nothing. You dream not because you are 'somebody' but because you are a 'nobody' and want to become a 'somebody'. So it is alright to dream big in small places. The size of the place in which you are does not matter; it is the size of the dream that matters.

You will also learn about the concept, purpose, power and principles governing dreams and the kind of person you must become in order to translate your dreams into reality. I want you to embark on the journey of discovering God's dream for your life and make it your dream. One of the few things that have not been monetized in this highly monetized economy is dreams. You do not need anything to dream -they are free. For example, If you think of attending a function in the London O2 Arena, you will also be thinking of the fee to pay, but if you are dreaming of owning the London O2 Arena one day, it will cost you nothing i.e. you pay nothing dreaming that big! You can dream big in small places.

CHAPTER 2

UNDERSTANDING DREAMS AND GOD'S CREATIVE PROCESS

DREAMS ATTRACT RESOURCES. THE GREATEST ASSET IN THE HANDS OF A MAN IS HIS DREAM.

Everything begins with a dream. Dreams are the genesis of civilization. Every great human achievement began as a dream. Dreams precede great works of art. Dreams precede a life that transforms other lives. Dreams precede groundbreaking revelations and revolutions. Dreams precede the establishment of great ministries or churches. Dreams precede the production of block buster movies. Dreams preceded the creation of every wonder of the earth. Dreams precede the building of families. Dreams have preceded the raising of godly and responsible children. All of human development is premised on dreams.

Show me a poor man and I will show you a man who is either without a dream or is not pursuing a dream. Show me a destitute man and I will show you a man with little dreams. Show me a poor country and I will show you a nation of people wallowing in the poverty of their imaginations and dreamlessness.

Show me a man beaten down by life and I will show you a man who is not yet convicted by his dreams. Show me a man stagnating at the same place for decades and I will show you a man struggling to translate his dreams into reality.

Show me a business that has remained at the same size and growth level for decades and I will show you one that lacks the ability and courage to dream lofty dreams.

An African-American leader Jesse Jackson said, "*If my eyes can see it, if my mind can conceive it, and my heart can believe it, I know I can achieve it.*" See it, conceive it, believe it and you will achieve it. That is why I agree with Helen Keller who said, "*The most pathetic person in the world is someone who has sight but has no vision.*" The poorest person is not just the man who lives on less than a dollar a day but also the man without a dream. ***The greatest hindrance to living is dreamlessness.*** The life of a man with a dream especially a God inspired dream is richer than a man without a dream who has inherited wealth or won the lottery.

Helen Keller also said that, it is better to have a dream and have no eye-sight than to have eye-sight without a dream. Dreamers have eyesight and mind-sight. Dreamers are both lookers and seers. Dreamers do not just have images passing through their mind in their sleep; they also have images of the future downloaded into their spirit and mind during the day.

As a pastor, I acknowledge the importance of the dreams of the night, but I also know the importance of the dreams we have when we are awake.

Dreams are like the photo studio where mental images are processed. Dreams are like the manufacturing centers where things are made. Dreams are like the software that powers computers. Dreams are like the kitchen where international cuisines are prepared. They all are first in the dream state before they become tangible things.

Dreams of the Night- God's Channel

Dreams have been God's communication channel since time of old. After the fall of man, when God no longer communicated with man directly, the mode of communication He has mostly used is the dreams we have when asleep. He spoke to the patriarchs, prophets, priests and kings through dreams. By dreams of the night, I am referring to the images, thoughts and emotions that pass through the mind during sleep. This is to be contrasted from the images and thoughts of the future that pass through our mind when we are wide awake.

The first instance of dreams of the night are introduced in the Bible in Genesis 15:12-21 where God revealed the future of Abraham's seed and gave him promises as well.

"Now when the sun was going down, <u>a deep sleep fell upon Abram; and behold, horror and great darkness fell upon him.</u>

Then He said to Abraham: "Know certainly that your descendants will be strangers in a land that is not theirs, and will serve them, and they will afflict them four hundred years.

And also the nation whom they serve I will judge; afterward they shall come out with great possessions". Genesis 15:12-14

In the passage above, there is no mention of the word 'dream'. However, since the Bible mentions that Abraham fell into a deep sleep and heard the voice of God in his sleep, it is obvious that he was dreaming. God was speaking to him about the future of his seed. Besides Abraham, these men - Isaac, Jacob, Joseph and Moses all experienced God speaking to them in their dreams. In the New Testament, God spoke to several people through dreams like Paul.

God confirmed in Numbers 12:6 that dreams are one of His communication channels with man.

"Then He said, 'Hear now My words: if there is a prophet among you, I, the LORD, make myself known to him in a

vision; I speak to him in a dream".

So dreams are one of the channels through which He speaks to man; it is one of God's telephone conversations with man. If you want to hear from God and know what He is doing and about to do, then take dreams seriously. For this book however, my focus is not on the dreams of the night. There is a second type of dream which I want to elucidate on.

The Second Type of Dream

The second type of dream is similar to the first type but different in some respects. Dreams are *"a cherished hope, an ambition or aspiration".* The hopes, ambitions and aspirations you cherish so much are dreams. This means when you mention hopes, ambitions and aspirations, it is synonymous to dreams and so can be used interchangeably. Thus, dreams are what you are *looking forward to with desire and reasonable confidence. It is an earnest desire for some type of achievement or distinction.* These desires you are looking forward to are in your mind and heart in the form of images and thoughts.

James Allen wrote that *"Dream lofty dreams, and as you dream, so you shall become. **Your vision is the promise of what you shall one day be; your ideal is the prophecy of what you shall at last unveil***". Your dream is the promise of what you shall one day be. It is YOU in the future – who you will be, what you will be doing, how you will be a blessing in the lives of people, how blessed you will be, where you will be. It is the promise you hold in the future. It is becoming all that God created you to be, accomplishing all that you were created to accomplish and having all that you were created to have. It is the vision of possibilities for your future and the promise of your future. Dreams are the mental images of your future as designed by God.

CHAPTER 3

THE THREE MOST IMPORTANT THINGS TO HAVE

BEFORE YOU PRIDE YOURSELF IN ANY MAJOR DISCOVERY, CHECK ITS IMPORTANCE AGAINST THE LAWS OF FAITH, HOPE AND LOVE.

I have established above that dreams are *"a cherished hope, an ambition or aspiration"*. Since dreams also mean hope, then dreams were inclusive in what the Apostle Paul wrote about in 1 Corinthians 13:13. I love the New International Reader's Version better:

*"The three most important things to have are faith, **hope** and love. And the greatest of these is love."*

This scripture can be rephrased as:

*"The three most important things to have are faith, **dreams** and love. And the greatest of these is love."*

God considers dreams to be one of the greatest things to have alongside faith and love. Dreams are that important to God; so important that He includes them in the list of the three most important things to have. Dreams are a part of the top three most important things to have. Life without dreams is no life at all.

It is better to start life without money and material things but with a dream than to start life with money thrown all at you but with no dream. In the story of the prodigal son, he inherited a lot of money but he could not make much of it because he did not have a personal and responsible dream that will enable him put the money to good use. Money is of no use when a man lacks a true dream. Money is valuable but in the hands of a man without a dream, it loses its value. When you have money without dreams, you dissipate the money. When you have dreams but no money, money will eventually flow to you. Since dreams are one of the three most important things in life, when you have them, they make you important. Lose your dream and lose your importance in life.

Another scripture which relates to dreams is Psalms 37:4 David wrote that,

"Delight yourself also in the LORD, and he shall give you the **desires** *of your heart."*

As I mentioned earlier, dreams are what you are looking forward to with desire. Every dream is a desire of the heart. Marilyn Manson wrote that *"When all of your wishes are granted, many of your dreams will be destroyed."* Why? Because your dreams are largely your wishes or desires. Not every desire is necessarily a God-given dream but every dream is made up of desires. With this understanding, we can rephrase Psalm 37:4 to read like this:

*"Delight yourself also in the LORD, and he shall give you the **dreams** of your heart."*

Delighting yourself in God means you take pleasure in God or enjoy being with God. When you take pleasure in God and the things of God, He steps in to help you fulfill your dreams. This also means God is interested in your dreams and knows their significance in your life - that the achievement of your dreams enhances your value and worth.

The above text also means God has an interest in everything about you and your dreams are a very significant part of you. Your dreams refine you today and define your tomorrow.

There are so many desires we have as rational beings. In talking about dreams, we are not referring to just something you wish for temporarily. It is not something you see someone pursue and gets you to say I would like to have that. It must be drawn out of your inner most being.

Your God-given Dream is Sourced From...

- The desires that burn in your heart like fire.

- The ideas that never leave your mind and keep coming back.

- The things you will commit your life to if you had all the resources in the world.

- The thing you believe strongly is God's specific purpose for your life.

- That thing you are doing alongside your regular job because you cannot let it go.

- That thing you want to achieve before you go home to be with Lord.

- That thing you have a natural flair for.

- That thing you hear a still small voice whispering into your ear to pursue.

CHAPTER 4

GOD IS A DREAMER

THE COMPLEX AND YET VIVIDLY ORDERED NATURE OF OUR WORLD IS A CLUE THAT SOMEONE TOOK TIME TO PLAN IT.

God is a dreamer because He has hopes and desires. He is not aspiring to be better because He is the best already. He does not have ambitions to have more because all things were created by Him. However, His hopes are all geared towards establishing His Kingdom on earth. His primary desire is to have as many people as possible accept Jesus and then live the Kingdom Life on earth. The well-being of His people is His dream now. Jeremiah 29:11 mentions this:

"For I know the thoughts that I think toward you, says the LORD, thoughts of peace and not of evil, to give you a future and a hope."

God has thoughts about us; He has images passing through His mind about you and He says these thoughts are about giving us a future and hope. God dreams about us; we are at the center of His existence. Everything He does is geared towards our well-being. The desires of God for us are still work in progress so God is still dreaming. In addition, God is a dreamer because He is the creator of the heavens and the earth. Every creator dreams before he creates anything. He carries the thoughts about what he wants to create before he creates them. God had to conceive how he wanted each one of us to be before bringing us into existence.

In creating us in His image, He deposited in us the ability to create which is why we have the ability to dream like He does.

Paul taught about the same thing in 1 Corinthians 2:9-10 when he wrote to the Corinthian church that:

"But as it is written: 'Eye has not seen, nor ear heard, nor have entered into the heart of man the things which God has prepared for those who love Him'

But God has revealed them to us through His Spirit. For the Spirit searches all things, yes, the deep things of God." (NIV)

From this scripture, we learn that God has some things He has prepared for those who love Him. God has prepared some things for everyone on this planet. What we need to do is discover the things He has prepared for us and make the attainment of those things part of our dream. Since God has prepared some things for us, it means there is a set vision in the heart of God about you but you need the Spirit to discern. Your dream should be founded on the things God has prepared for you and can mainly be discovered through a revelation by the Holy Spirit.

God Speaks Through Dreams of the Heart and Mind

Earlier on, I mentioned what God said through Moses - that He speaks to His prophets through dreams and visions. In that scripture, the dreams He was talking about is the one we have when asleep. The truth is, God does not only speak to us when we are asleep, He also speaks when we are awake. He does not only speak through the dreams of the night but also through our hopes, ambitions and aspirations.

The pastor of the largest church in the world, Pastor Yonghi Cho confirms this when he said, *"the language of the Holy Spirit is in dreams, visions and ideas."* The Holy Spirit speaks to us through our dreams – that is, our hopes, ambitions and aspirations. Successful Brazilian author and lyricist Paulo Coelho also said *"Dreams are the language of God."* There are a lot of great projects accomplished by people which begun as a strong desire planted in their hearts by God. They did not see a spiritual vision; they did not dream at night, they did not hear the audible voice of God or receive a message from a prophet. God simply deposited the desire in their hearts.

In Philippians 2:13, Paul confirms this when he wrote;

*"(Not in your own strength) for it is God Who is all the while effectually at work in you **(energizing and creating in you the power and desire), both to will** and to work for His good pleasure and satisfaction and delight".* (Amplified Version)

We learn from the above scripture that God implants desires in our hearts so that we will do things that bring Him pleasure, satisfaction and delight. When you are born again and have the Spirit of God living in you, He implants some strong desires in your heart about your future. Do not ignore every desire rather be sensitive to the Holy Spirit. I know of Christians who will not pursue a particular God- birthed desire until they receive a vision, a prophetic word or other revelation. But it is not everyone God speaks to through these revelation gifts. If He does not, it does not mean He is not speaking to you. Do not limit God in the ways He speaks.

In the book of Job, we learn of how God implants dreams in the hearts of men.

"For God may speak in one way, or another; yet man does not perceive it.

In a dream, in a vision of the night, when deep sleep falls upon men, while slumbering on their beds, then He opens the ears of men, And seals their instruction." Job 33:14-16

This passage teaches that God speaks in more than one way to man. In verse 15, he goes on to talk about how God speaks in dreams and visions of the night and how He opens our ears and slots in instructions when we fall into deep sleep. I believe that there are three independent ways (dreams, visions of the night and slotting in instructions through our ears) God reveals His will to us.

What does it mean to receive instructions through the ears whilst asleep? This sounds like God leaves a recorded message in your spirit to wake up to. He opens our ears and inserts, slots or seals an instruction into us. Thus, you wake up to a fresh idea, creative concept and a new desire you want to pursue. Another characteristic of this is the calm assurance and confidence you have that it is of God and can be achieved. When something is sealed, it implies it is secured, locked up or closed in. Though it was slotted into your spirit whilst you were asleep, it was not necessarily images or pictures that passed through your mind but rather a spiritual instruction that drives you to the place of achievement.

A good analogy is in the creation of Eve. Adam was put into a deep sleep. Whilst he slept, God performed a surgery on him, removed some of his ribs and used it to create the woman. When Adam awoke, God brought the woman to Adam and immediately he knew who Eve was and he was excited about her. Whilst Adam slept; God was preparing something for him. In some of our moments of sleep, God prepares us to achieve certain things by making implants into our spirits.

Just as God performed a physical surgery on Adam, He can also perform a spiritual surgery on us. In the case of Adam, He removed a rib from him but in our case, He makes an implant into our spirits. The conviction that made Adam say "This is now bone of my bones and flesh of my flesh" is the same that happens when the idea or instruction you have received from God synchronizes well with your soul.

God Gives A Dream When He Calls You

When God called Abraham in Genesis 12, He told him He was going to make him into a great nation, bless him, make his name great and make him a blessing; he was giving him something to make the dream of his life.

"Now the Lord had said unto Abraham...I will make of thee a great nation, and I will bless thee and make thy name great; and thou shall be a blessing. And I will bless them that bless thee: and curse them that curse thee: and in thee shall all families of the earth be blessed". Genesis 12:1-3.

When he told him that his descendants would be as many as the stars in the sky and the dust of the earth, He was planting a dream in him. When God called Moses and told him He was going to use him to deliver the Israelites from Egypt and take them to a good land, a land flowing with milk and honey, He was giving him a dream. When God called David to be king of Israel through Prophet Samuel, He was giving him a dream.

Whenever God calls you, a dream follows. He never calls you without giving you a dream. Your dream must be sourced from God's call or purpose for your life. The fact that you may not have found God's dream for your life does not mean it does not exist. Find God's dream for your life today and pursue it.

God's Glorious Dream For You is Predestined

In Romans 8:29-30, Paul reveals God's intent for mankind, the ultimate purpose He has in mind for us and the stages He takes us through to arrive at this end. According to this passage, the stages are foreknowledge, predestination, calling, justification and glorification.

*"For whom He **foreknew**, He also **predestined** to be conformed to the image of His Son, that He might be the firstborn among many brethren.*

*Moreover whom He predestined, these He also **called;** whom He called, these He also **justified**; and whom He justified, these He also **glorified.**"*

The final stage in this 5-stage process is glory. The end God is dreaming for us is one of glorification. He dreams of a life that ends in glory and not shame; fulfillment of dreams and not failure. A glorious life is God's dream for you. He created you for glory. Your dream should be a manifestation of the glory God desires for you. The fulfillment of your dream should glorify God.

There are four steps that lead to fulfilling God's dream of glory for your life. The first step is Foreknowledge. Foreknowledge is to know something before it happens. It implies God knew you before you were conceived and born. Remember, He is the Alpha and the Omega so He knows the beginning and the end. That is what He meant when He told Jeremiah that "before I formed you in the mother's womb, I knew you." God knows your glorious end right from your beginning. He knew you before you started life. No matter the condition surrounding your birth, you are not an after-thought. Do not allow the enemy to talk you into thinking God does not think or care about you.

The second stage is Predestination. After knowing about you before conception, He predetermined the kind of life you will live before you were born. Predestination is synonymous to what God said to Jeremiah that "I had appointed you to be a prophet to the nations." Predestination means God planned for you to be a particular person and to do a particular work. It is one thing for a parent to expect a baby and another thing to plan the life of the baby before birth. Not every parent plans for their baby. But God is different; He planned and prepared for you before you were born.

What kick-starts the predestined plan is the call of God. The call of God begins the implementation or roll out of all that He has predetermined for you. This call is twofold – it is a call to accept Christ as Savior and Lord and a call to fulfill His specific purpose for your life. When you respond positively to God's call, you are justified. The third step is Justification.

Justification comes about through believing in Christ. As long as you arrive at this stage, your glorious life is in view; God's dream for you will come to pass. "...and whom He justified, these He also glorified." If you have responded to the call of God, then you automatically qualify for the fourth step - which is Glorification. Glorification is the aspect where God significantly beautifies and decorates your life as His own showpiece of Glory.

God Goes Beyond Our Dreams

Ephesians 3:20 is one of the rich verses in scripture:

"Now to Him who is able to do exceedingly abundantly above all that we ask or think, according to the power that works in us".

This scripture reveals that God can do more than we ask or think. Dreams are a part of what we think. God can beat us to our dreams. As He spoke through the Prophet Isaiah in Isaiah 55:8-9:

"For my thoughts are not your thoughts, nor are your ways my ways, says the LORD.

For as the heavens are higher than the earth, so are my ways higher than your ways, and my thoughts than your thoughts."

The Big Dream Factor

God's thoughts which include His thoughts concerning us and our future are higher and bigger than ours. God is a big thinker. The vastness of the earth is a reflection of His big thinking. Oral Roberts understood this so he had in his office at the Oral Roberts University, an inscription that read: "Make no little plans here". Your God is a big God so do not dream small.

Though God beats our imagination, our dreams are still His raw materials for our future. They are inputs He takes into consideration when He has to do anything in your life. Even when He has to set it aside for something higher, He still will give you a better dream and meet some other delights of your heart. Your dreams serve as a blueprint for God's input into your future. Like a painter conceives in His mind what He wants to paint before he starts painting, so does God draw on the images we have in our mind, improve on them and use it to paint our future/destiny for us.

We Are in an Era of Dreams and Visions

One characteristic of the last days is that, "...*the people that do know their God shall be strong, and do exploits*" (Daniel 11:32b). We are in an era where the knowledge of God is increasing, birthing spiritual strength and great achievements. He is set to do great things that will be a blessing to people and make history, all geared towards causing His kingdom to come on earth and revealing His glory. Jesus also said that if we believe in Him, we shall do greater works than what He did. Greater manifestations and works are a part of God's end-time agenda. But as His principle is, He does nothing without revealing it to His servants the prophets (Amos 3:7). Everything God wants to do on earth, He must reveal it to His people and work through them to achieve it.

The revelation of the great works He wants to do is a part of what the Prophet Joel prophesied about in Joel 2:28;

"And it shall come to pass afterward that I will pour out My Spirit on all flesh; your sons and your daughters shall prophesy, your old men shall dream dreams, your young men shall see visions." Joel 2:28

Since dreams precede great achievements, God has to reveal part of His thoughts to us through prophecy, dreams and visions. The dreams referred to here is not restricted to the dreams we have at night only but the dreams He implants in our hearts and minds when we are awake. We are in an era of dreams and visions and anyone connected to the Holy Spirit must be inspired with dreams from God. He will give you dreams about family, career, business and ministry.

CHAPTER 5

GOD'S CREATIVE PRINCIPLE: THE UNSEEN REALM AND THE SEEN REALM

IT IS ALWAYS INTERESTING TO KNOW THAT IT IS THE UNSEEN THAT BIRTHS THE SEEN.

Now faith is the substance of things hoped for, the evidence of things not seen.

For by it the elders obtained a good testimony.

"By faith we understand that the worlds were framed by the word of God, so that the things which are seen were not made of things which are visible." Hebrews 11:1-3

In the third verse above, we are told that the worlds were created by the Word of God. The worlds here refer to the universe – the planet earth, all other celestial bodies including other planets and everything in it, both living and non-living. The Word of God is the spoken word as recorded in Genesis during the story of creation. The

Apostle Paul again went on to say *"the things which are seen are not made of things which are visible".* In other words, the things which are seen were made from the things which are not seen. The spoken Word of God which cannot be seen created the world. This means God used invisible things to create visible things; unseen things to create seen things; spiritual things to create natural or physical things.

Beyond that, how about the things which man has created? Do they also follow the same principle? Definitely! I believe that the visible things man has created were also made from things which are not seen and these things we do not see include dreams, visions and ideas. Dreams, visions and ideas are not seen with our physical eyes yet they create the things we see. The mind cannot be seen yet from it come visions and ideas which are conceived and later birthed. This is the process for creating things.

This process means that , buildings, products, equipments or organizations are not built from the things we see. Buildings are not made from just physical materials such as sand and cement. Scientific inventions are not invented from resources we can see around us.

Napoleon Hill wrote that *"Man, alone, has the power to transform his thoughts into physical reality; man, alone, can dream and make his dreams come true."* What we term *'reality'* is that which is tangible. Thoughts are not tangible and he says it is only man who can transform his thoughts (intangible things) into tangible things. Intangible things like thoughts create tangible things.

Since the creator is more important than the creature, the unseen is more important than the seen, the invisible realm is more important than the visible realm and the spiritual more than the natural. So dreams, ideas, thoughts are more important than physical things because they create those physical things.

People who know how to live in the world of the unseen – the world of dreams, visions, ideas, beliefs, knowledge and wisdom succeed in the real world. Value them. You need to have these people in your life. Do not live in your memory, live in your imagination. Think about the future; do not worry about the past.

The Principle of Double Creation

Everything you see was created twice. The first creation happens in the mind of the creator. The second creation is when what is in the mind is brought into reality. Everything you see around you was first in the mind of a person before you saw or experienced it. I believe it is a universal principle which works for you, whether you are a believer or not. God works with this universal principle as He revealed in Jeremiah 1:4-5;

"Then the word of the LORD came to me, saying:

Before I formed you in the womb I knew you; before you were born I sanctified you; I ordained you a prophet to the nations."

Here, God says He knew Jeremiah before he was formed in his mother's womb. How can you know someone before he was born? Before he was born, he was invisible, in fact intangible. He definitely did not exist and yet God says He knew him. How possible can it be that you know something before it came into existence? Through the principle of double creation. We existed in what I choose to call the Spirit World before we came into being. The Spirit World created the natural world.

Before anything comes into existence, it actually exists but in another realm or world. It exists in you, in your mind and heart in the form of dreams, ideas and thoughts. The places where dreams, ideas and thoughts exist are a world on their own. I call it the Thought World and it creates the material world.

Read what Vera Nazarian wrote:

"One of the strangest things is the act of creation. You are faced with a blanket slate – a page, a canvas, a block of stone or wood, a silent musical instrument.

You then look inside yourself. You pull and tug and squeeze and fish around for slippery raw shapeless things that swim like fish made of cloud vapor and fill you with living clamor. You latch onto something. And you bring it forth out of your head like Zeus giving birth to Athena. And as it comes out, it takes shape and tangible form.

It drips on the canvas, and slides through your pen, it springs forth and resonates into the musical strings, and slips along the edge of the sculptor's tool onto the surface of the wood or marble.

You have given it cohesion. You have brought forth something ordered and beautiful out of nothing. You have glimpsed the divine."

Everything man has created was created from nothing. Form begins as formlessness; something comes from nothing; shape out of shapelessness; greatness out of smallness. When you dream, the thing you dream about is non-existent, yet we add bone to bone, flesh to flesh, sinews to sinews and connect one thing to another giving the dream a life of its own. As Vera points out, when a work of art is done, it is a process where *"you have brought forth something ordered and beautiful out of nothing."*

A Word document may be blank but the mind of the author is never blank. The potter's wheel may not be turning but the potter's mind is churning. The painter's canvas may have no drop of paint but his mind is pregnant with new painting. The keyboard may be yet to be played but the fingers of the pianist always have some music in them. This is because the book, the pottery, the painting or the music already exists in a certain form in the mind of the creator.

There is always another painting in the mind of the painter; another design in the mind of the designer; another fashion line in the mind of the fashion designer; another sculpture in the mind of the sculptor; another goal in the mind of the prolific football striker; another book in the mind of the author; another winning case in the mind of the lawyer; another song in the musician; another app in the mind of the software developer. Apple is coming up with another device; Microsoft will be launching another version of Windows next year and it goes on and on and on. When you are born to be a particular person and to do something, you are never finished, you are never empty and you are never done.

That's why you should not stop dreaming; do not stop hoping. As Paul said, *"Now these three remain: faith, hope and love".* When all else fails you and you lose all that you have worked for, the things that must remain in your life are faith, hope and love. All else may fail but don't fail to dream. The dreams you hold in your area of calling, your assignment, purpose and destiny should remain. The things God spoke to you about your future through His word, through the inner witness/conviction, through that dream, vision or prophecy should remain.

CHAPTER 6

THE POWER OF MEDITATION

EVERY TIME YOU IMAGINE, YOU GIVE YOUR SOUL AN ASSIGNMENT.

Psalm 119:97 "Oh how love I thy law! It is my meditation all the day."

What are you meditating on? Meditation simply means to engage in thought or contemplation – to reflect. Beloved, know for sure that at every moment, you are creating something new. This is because you are always brooding over, desiring, expecting or hoping for something. The issue is what are you brooding over in your mind? You will definitely birth what you continuously brood over. No wonder Solomon said "for as a man thinketh in his heart so is he..." Proverbs 23:7. Again, Jesus said if you look at a woman lustfully you have already committed adultery with her in your heart.

*"But I say unto you, that whosoever **looketh on a woman to lust after her hath** committed adultery with her already in his heart."* Mathew 5:28.

"Looketh on a woman to lust after her" is as much as meditating or pondering on the act of committing adultery with her; in other words, you are dreaming of having her. Jesus is saying dreaming of having her is equal to having her physically. The principle here is what you create in your mind is as good as real. Beware of what you constantly meditate on!

The Power of Visualization

In Genesis 30:37-39, Jacob adopted a practice which is laden with insights on how to birth what one desires.

"Jacob, however, took fresh-cut branches from poplar, almond and plane trees and made white stripes on them by peeling the bark and exposing the white inner wood of the branches.

Then he placed the peeled branches in all the watering troughs, so that they would be directly in front of the flocks when they came to drink. When the flocks were in heat and came to drink,

They mated in front of the branches. And they bore young that were streaked, speckled or spotted."

The idea above was received through a dream from God. It was a God-given idea. Jacob peeled the back of branches of an almond, poplar and plane trees to expose the inner part of the branch which is white. Then he placed them at all the places where the flock drink from (and flocks drink water very frequently). It means they always saw the inner white portion of the wood when they drank water and when they mated. As long as this continued especially during their mating season, the animals conceived and gave birth to young ones which were streaked, speckled or spotted.

They bore this color of young not because they (the male flock) were spotted but because they continually saw the inner white portion of the wood when they were mating. As long as it was in front of them, they conceived. What they conceived was based on what their eyes saw. Though this is an idea that worked in animal rearing, it contains a proven principle for realizing ones dreams.

An African-American leader Jesse Jackson said that, "*If my eyes can see it, if my mind can conceive it, and my heart can believe it, I know I can achieve it.*" The beginning of achievement is visualization. What you can visualize and keep in your imagination, you can actualize. He says here that what you see is what you will conceive. If you do not see it, you will not conceive it.

The "Jacobic" Principle of Reproduction

This principle works not only through having a dream but placing images or pictures of what you want to achieve before you. What Jacob did was to put before the flock, pictures of the color he wanted the young who were born to bear.

Get a picture of your dream life – achievement, lifestyle, family, business, career, house or car - any picture that reflects the future you desire and have it before you every day. Jacob placed it in the watering troughs so the flock saw it frequently. Put it at where you can never miss it in any day; a place where you spend most of your day. It could be beside your dressing mirror in your bedroom or at the mirror at the sink where you brush your teeth every morning. The image you continually see and conceive in your mind and believe in your heart is what will manifest in your life.

It could also be the environment you are exposed to. The environment the flock dwelt in was full of these almond branches with their back peeled and so they conceived something their environment was replete with. Your environment can influence what you dream and achieve. At times what you need is a change of environment because what you are conceiving is from your environment and is not in alignment with God's dream for you.

In placing the peeled branches in the watering troughs, he was altering their environment. Altering your environment can be either taking something from your environment or adding something to it. Jacob added something to the flock's environment. There could be something in your environment that discourages you, clouds your judgment or pulls you back. Alter your environment to push you closer to your dream. Your environment must help the fulfillment of your dream and not hurt it.

CHAPTER 7

DOWNLOADING HEAVEN ONTO THE EARTH

GOD HAS GIVEN TO EVERY MAN THE POWER TO INVOLVE HEAVEN IN HIS EARTHLY AFFAIRS.

I have learnt by revelation that there are some things on earth with greater and better equivalence in Heaven. Remember that Heaven is a place of perfection and everything in Heaven is at the peak of perfection, completeness or in its best state ever. There is a better version of the peace of God which surpasses all understanding in Heaven. There is a better version of the joy of the Holy Ghost in Heaven. There are better riches in Heaven than what exists on earth.

After this life, there will be a new city where qualified Christians will be living according to the book of Revelation:

"And I saw a new heaven and a new earth: for the first heaven and the first earth were passed away; and there was no more sea.

*And I John saw the **holy city,** new Jerusalem, coming down from God out of heaven, prepared as a bride adorned for her husband."* Revelations 21:1-2

There are cities on this current earth and there will be a city coming from the new Heaven where we will reside. Note that when God created the world in the beginning, there was no mention of city. He simply created a garden and placed man there. The new city that is going to be created will have walls and gates built of precious stones and minerals with streets of gold. There is no city on this current earth that has its streets made of gold and all walls made of precious stones but later in the next earth, the streets will be made of gold.

"And the twelve gates were twelve pearls; every several gate was of one pearl: and the street of the city was pure gold, as it was transparent glass."

Revelations 21:21

The Eden factor

When God created the world in the beginning, from the account and description in Genesis, He created the Garden of Eden. He did not create a city. He did not build walls in

Eden; He created a garden with trees and flowers. He did not create streets, He only created soils, mountains and precious minerals out of which man has created streets. It will also amaze you that some of the things man has created on earth will be found in Heaven. The literature genius William Shakespeare wrote *"There are more things in Heaven and earth... than are dreamt of in your philosophy."* Now, the things which man has created here on earth, which have their equivalent in heaven were not originally created by God for man on earth. The big question is how was man able to catch the vision of heaven and create them on earth?

The Jesse Duplantis Encounter

Let me share with you an excerpt from a book by an American preacher Jesse Duplantis of Jesse Duplantis Ministries on some heavenly encounters he had. The book is titled, *'Heaven: Close Encounters of the God Kind.'* On pages 74–76, he talks about a visit to heaven and he was privileged to have King David take him around some places in heaven including his house in heaven.

"I Saw My House in Heaven."

*Then he took me to **my house**. When I walked up, I looked at the grounds. There was a **water fountain** in the front yard and manicured grass. It was the prettiest place I had ever* laid eyes on. I said, 'This is my house?'

'Yes,' David said. 'Would you like to go inside?'

'Yes, I want to go inside!'

To me, the foyer of a home sets the mood of a house. When I went through the front door, there were **tall ceilings and crown moldings**.

'Do you like it?' David asked.

'Yes I like it. This is beautiful!' Everything was decorated and the **furniture** was just the kind I liked. I said, 'This place is beautiful! I wasn't expecting to see this. Just look at this place! **Hey, I have furniture like that on the earth**! I love this!'

'Yes, the Lord knew you would like it, so we put it in your home. We told you He would give you the desires of your heart, David said.

'All desires are met here. Everything has been thought of - all your desires and some that you could not even think of.'

Everything was perfect down to the last detail! It was so beautiful! I looked at more physical things in my home than anywhere else. There was marble, and there was a table in the foyer with golden eagles on it! I said, 'Look at this!'

'**David,' I said, 'there are lots of things here that look like things on earth.'**

'**Well, the earth is the Lord's taste,' he answered. 'Remember, He created it. So a lot of what you see there you will see here.**

Come let me show you more.'

'The thing that bothers me, David, is that I never thought there would be things here like mountains.'

'Jesse, the earth is God's creation. His taste there is His taste here.'"

There are houses with foyer, water fountains, tall ceilings, crown moldings and furniture in heaven. If God did not create furniture but created trees, then how come Jesse Duplantis had some of the furniture on earth also in his house in heaven? How come there are things on earth which can be found in Heaven but were not things created by God originally? How did they get to the earth? We are not told anywhere in scripture how such natural things came about. I believe that the same creative ability through which God created the world is the same ability we have used to create artificial things. The same creative process through which God created the world is the same process through which man has created artificial things to improve our way of living.

You Were Created To Create

Some people are of the opinion that every material thing man has created is demonic. If they are evil and demonic, there would not be a finer version of them in Heaven. I believe that when God said, *"let us make man in our own image that he may have dominion...."* the ability to have dominion was implanted in us. This ability included the ability to create things. When He blessed man and commanded man to be fruitful and multiply it was not just about biological fruitfulness but also about creating things to fill the earth and meet our needs.

The earth is the Lord's taste. Some of the things in Heaven, He did not create on earth directly for us, rather He has enabled man to create those things. God enables us by implanting desires, hopes, ambitions and expectations in the minds and hearts of men to improve on life. These dreams often come in the form of ideas and thoughts and it is when they are translated into reality that they become things we benefit from. I believe that there are things in heaven for which God gives dreams to man to create earthly versions of them for our own use. God does that as a good God with the intention of improving our way of living. Through dreams, we are able to download heaven onto the earth. Through dreams, the kingdom of God is established on earth.

CHAPTER 8

THE SOURCE, POWER AND TIME VALUE OF A DREAM

EVERY GOD GIVEN DREAM IS DESIGNED TO
OUTLAST THE PERSON THAT DREAMT IT.

Everyone dreams. The ability to dream and translate it into reality is a universal ability peculiar to man only. Napoleon Hill wrote that ". We have the freedom and permission to dream about anything we want. The things that are permissible and lawful for every human being to do includes dreaming.

The ability to dream and realize the dream is independent of a person's spirituality or character. An atheist can dream and realize them as much as a Christian. An immoral person can also dream and realize them. In fact, to be an atheist or an immoral person all flows from the thoughts, the images or desires the person conceives. When you accept thoughts or images about the non-existence of

God, then you become an atheist. When you entertain thoughts and images about immoral things, then you will become immoral. Every state of a man is dreamt of before he lives it. Every dream has the potential to come to pass irrespective of the source and the content.

Osama bin Laden had dreams. He is quoted to have said, *"I'm fighting so I can die a martyr and go to heaven to meet God. Our fight now is against the Americans."* He also said elsewhere that *"We treat them in the same way. Those who kill our women and innocent, we kill their women and innocent, until they refrain."* His dream included killing Americans and that is not a dream God endorses. Hitler also had dreams and achieved some of this dreams. But would you say every dream of these men were of God? Definitely not!

The Inspiration of Your Dreams

Just as God can inspire a dream in your spirit, the enemy can also do same. He is an imitator of God. Because the process of creation is a universal principle, the enemy also takes advantage of this to make men work for him. The dreams of people like Osama bin Laden and Hitler were inspired by the devil himself and not God.

For believers, he can sow dreams in our hearts and minds with the purpose of deviating them from God's divine destiny. The dreams of God for you are the best you can get. What the enemy does at times is to give you a dream that is a good one but not God's best for you. The enemy knows that if he inspires one that is conspicuously contrary to God's word, you will easily know it's not from God. What he does then, is to dilute or divert the dream so to prevent you from God's best for you. In fact, a dream may sound good but it may not be of God. A good dream is not necessarily a 'God dream'. It may sound good to you and other people but it may not sound good to God.

Dreams can also be inspired by our selfish desires or lusts. The dreams that will create eternal treasures for you are the dreams that are birthed from God's word through His Spirit. Your dream must have a connection to Heaven; it should be aligned to God's eternal purpose for mankind and His prophetic purpose concerning your life. If your dream is to wear the best designer suit, eat every meal like a king, drive the latest car, live in a multi-million dollar mansion and become famous, you could still be the most pitiful person on earth. Your dream will be of no eternal value because it is all about you and does not mention how you want to benefit and give to others.

The Power of Dreams

Dreams Are The Compass of Your Life

During the Second World War, German submarines usually targeted enemy ships and caused them to sink by shooting

61

at them. In 1942, Russian immigrant and junior engineer Semenov was on the American merchant ship, SS Alcoa Guide which was sailing from New Jersey to Guadeloupe, a Caribbean island. *"On the night of April 16, about 300 miles east of Cape Hatteras, North Carolina, a German submarine, the U-123, surfaced and opened fire with its deck cannon. We didn't have any guns, and there was no escort,"* Semenov recalls. *"We didn't have much speed. They used us as target practice."*

They got off the boat and *"Using the small compass on the lifeboat, the survivors sailed west by northwest toward the shipping lanes. After three days, a patrol plane, searching for sailors from any of the half-dozen ships sunk that week, spotted Semenov's lifeboat. The next day, after a night of heavy rain, the American destroyer USS* Broome *rescued the men and soon picked up the other lifeboat and its survivors"* (http://www.smithsonianmag.com/arts-culture/Object-at-Hand-Ships-Compass).

The survival of these sailors was largely influenced by their use of the compass because it would have been difficult for them to know which direction was best for them to sail to without it.

As the compass was to the sailors, so do dreams do for us in the journey of life. Dreams give us direction for our life. When you conceive a dream, it directs you on what you should commit your life to, who you should commit your life to and where you should commit your resources.

Without a dream, you will not know which direction to take in life. As Henry David Thoreau said, *"Go confidently in the direction of your dreams. Live the life you've imagined".*

Dreams Give Meaning to Your Life

When you are young, immature and inexperienced, you look forward to the day that you will become independent, rich and successful. You look forward to living in a mansion, driving the latest car, wearing designer clothes or travelling around the world, thinking they will bring meaning to your life. I believe that as much as these things can be a part of your dream, they are not ultimate in terms of guaranteeing a meaning in life. Things are a means to an end not the end in themselves.

A true dream from God brings meaning to your life. It is about the end, purpose and significance of life. It gives you a reason to live which is higher than meeting your basic needs. It is not about what you want out of life but what you give to life. It is not what you want to become but what you want others to become. It is that which you were born to be and do.

Dreams Are The Fuel of Your Life

Dubai is one of the most beautiful, expensive and developed places in the world today. The economy of Dubai is built on the back of the oil economy. Today, however, they have diversified their developmental efforts and have concentrated on building their tourism, real estate, IT and finance credentials. But the fuel of Dubai's current status can be attributed to the discovery of oil in 1966. Oil was the fuel of the Dubai economy.

Dreams play a similar role in your life, in the same way as the fuel that contributed to the development of Dubai. They provide you with energy, drive and enthusiasm needed for you to live and thrive. If you are to live the kind of life God desires for you, you are going to need loads of passion, energy, drive and enthusiasm. Normal Vincent Peale wrote that *"The more you lose yourself in something bigger than yourself, the more energy you will have"*. When you focus on your dreams, they supply you with the energy to move closer to your destiny. When a car runs out of fuel, no matter how expensive, beautiful or sophisticated it is, it will not move. Without energy, you are going nowhere in life.

Dreams Are The Telescope of Your Life

A telescope is a device for making distant objects appear larger and therefore nearer. It has improved man's understanding of some celestial bodies. For a telescope to function properly, it has to be focused on one particular thing. When it is focused, it brings the object of focus nearer, clearer and larger though very far off.

Dreams function as telescopes; they enable us to focus on one particular thing in the future. When you focus on one thing in life, it brings it nearer, clearer and larger. Developments in our world today offer so many attractions to each of us and if you are not careful, you will scatter your efforts, time and resources all over because you are unable to concentrate on everything at the same time. But when you have a dream, your life is focused on who and what will contribute towards the realization of your dream.

Dreams Are a Measure of Your Life

A scale is used to measure weight. A watch or calendar is used to measure time. Rulers or a tape measure is used for length. A compass is used to measure a circle. There are ways of measuring several things in life. But have you asked yourself what do we use to measure our progress in life?

Dreams serve as one of the measures of the progress you are making in life. God measures our obedience amongst other things, by what we have done with what He created us to do. So life is wasted when we fail to discover God's dream for our life. You could be achieving a lot in life yet not in alignment with what God called you to do and so it becomes a poor measure of your life. There is a lot of wisdom in Jim Rohn's statement that, "*If someone is going down the wrong road, he doesn't need motivation to speed him up. What he needs is education to turn him around.*"

Insights From Jacob's Dream

In Genesis 28:10-13, God gave Jacob a promise and revealed his future to him in a dream. This was a dream that he had whiles asleep and which was to define his future. Let us read it and share some insights from it.

"Now Jacob went out from Beersheba and went toward Haran.

So he came to a certain place and stayed there all night, because the sun had set. And he took one of the stones of that place and put it at his head, and he lay down in that place to sleep.

Then he dreamed, and behold, a ladder was set up on the earth, and its top reached to heaven; and there the angels of God were ascending and descending on it.

And behold, the LORD stood above it and said: "I am the LORD God of Abraham your father and the God of Isaac; the land on which you lie I will give to you and your descendants."

In the dream, there was a ladder that was set up from the earth to heaven, angels were moving up and down on it and God was positioned on top of it.

Jacob's dream was from God. God will not give you a dream that is contrary to His Word. That is why the dreams of Osama and Hitler could not have been of God. The basic measure of the value of a dream is the word of God. What does God's word say about it? You cannot desire to be homosexual and say that is how God created you so there is nothing you can do about it apart from translating those desires into reality. That argument is like saying " I desire to steal and that is how I was created to be so I will go ahead and steal".

The source of Jacob's dream was God. It was not just from God, but also God was in it. God has to be in your dream. You need to allow Him to sow a dream in you and birth it through you as well. Some people receive dreams and disconnect from God who is the source of it all. No dream from God can be achieved to its peak without a close relationship. When God's dream becomes your dream, you give that dream eternal value. God has rewards for people who commit their lives to do what He instructs them to do. Some of the rewards are received here on earth and others in Heaven. Such dreams receive plaudits in Heaven and so gain eternal value. If you pursue dreams that do not count for God, His purpose for your life and that of mankind, your dream is of no eternal value. It will not earn you this commendation, *"well done, thou good and faithful servant"*. It might be of value to other people but it does not necessarily mean it is of great value to God. It may speak for you in this lifetime but may not speak for you in the next life where we will spend eternity.

God Should Be Placed Above Your Dream

In Jacob's dream, God was not just in the dream; He was on top of the ladder in the dream. The position of God must be above your dream; the dream should not be above God. God is bigger than your dreams. There is danger in loving your dreams more than the things that matter in life. Your dream can in no way compare with God. Your dreams are a part of life and not the total essence of your life. Your relationship with God is more important than your dreams. Do not sacrifice your relationship with God for your dreams. Remember, if you delight yourself in the Lord, He will give you the desires (dreams) of your heart.

CHAPTER 9

THE LIFESPAN OF DREAMS

ETERNITY WAS ONCE A DREAM.

If the dream is founded on God's Word or inspired by God, it will last as long as God desires it to. King Solomon said that:

"Whatever God does endures forever, nothing can be added to it, nor anything taken from it." Ecclesiastes 3:14

So in reality, the dream you pursue now will continue with you after death. The legacy you leave behind is based on the dream you are pursuing today.

You Were Created For Eternity

Eternity means forever; life without end. Can you imagine living forever? The highest mountain in the world is Everest. Imagine a little bird that comes round every year to pick a grain of sand from the Mount Everest till the mountain is no more. Even though the mountain is exhausted, eternity still exists. King Solomon wrote about it in Ecclesiastes 3:11;

"He has made everything beautiful in its time. Also, He has put eternity in their hearts, except that no one can find out the work that God does from beginning to end."

God created us with eternity in our hearts. That is why after death, there is still life that continues beyond. The real you, your spirit and soul do not die when your body does, they just change worlds. The existence of life after death is independent of your belief and preparedness. In other words, whether you believe it or not, there is an after-life and you will spend yours in one of the two places – Heaven or hell.

Time Is a Drop of Eternity

By Time, I am referring to the period we spend on this planet. Time is a fraction of eternity given to man to write a story about himself. Life on earth is nothing compared to life after death as we enter into the phase of eternal life. Even if you spend one hundred and twenty years on this earth it is nothing compared to eternity. It is like a second of time in the realms of eternity. You can be a visionary on earth but if you do not prepare for eternity, you have become short-sighted. Is your dream preparing you for life on earth only or life after earth as well?

The True Purpose of Time

This life is to prepare us for the next life. Life on this earth is what will determine life in Heaven. What I do today will determine who I become tomorrow. Wisdom therefore teaches that I should not spend my time on only things that pertain to this earthly time but on eternity as well. The dreams I hold today must cover my eternity. The dreams on earth must be an input into my dreams for eternity. They should prepare you for eternal life and not eternal damnation. Dreams must have value in time and eternity.

Building Treasures in Heaven

Everyone has an investment account in heaven and what you do on earth determines the value of your account in heaven. The security of your treasures is also determined by where you invest it. The most insecure place to store your treasures is on this earth because it will all pass away one day. Instead of investing all you have on earth, convert some into heaven's investment products. Heaven offers higher returns on the investments it receives than any investment bank on earth. Your dreams should be the kind that create Heavenly value for your existence.

When your dreams are related to making people seek the Kingdom of God and His righteousness, they gain eternal value. Every dream related to building the Kingdom of God in any way possible gets His commendation. Win souls for the Kingdom of God with your dreams. Contribute to the expansion of the Kingdom of God. Bring healing to the hurting, hope to the hopeless and salvation to the sinner. Feed the hungry, fill the thirsty soul and educate the ignorant with your dreams. Lighten the dark places of life with your dreams. Clothe the destitute, house the homeless, deliver the oppressed, break negative addictions prosper lives and put a smile on somebody's face - all with your dreams. Let your dreams not just bless you but also make you a blessing.

The Dream, The Place and The Man

When God spoke to Abraham about being the father of many nations, he was ninety years but had no child. When Jacob dreamt of God repeating the promise He gave to Abraham, he was sleeping in the middle of nowhere using a stone as a pillow. When God spoke to Moses that He was going to use him to deliver the Israelites out of Egypt to Canaan, he was a fugitive who had been on the run for about forty years. When the Israelites were told that they were being taken to a land flowing with milk and honey, they were slaves whose slave masters were not ready to let them go.

All these people received dreams which were way bigger than them and their life situation. Apart from the fact that God was on their side, they were not well positioned to realize those dreams. There is always a gap between the dream and the kind of person you are now. The dream is always bigger than you and very far from your current life situation. If you focus on the present reality, you can be discouraged. If you focus on the kind of person you are today in relation to the size of the dream, you may feel overwhelmed or intimidated. But as Martin Luther King said, *"Take the first step in faith. You don't have to see the whole staircase. Just take the first step."*

The Size of a Dream Reveals the Size of a Man

The size of a dream is a reflection of the person behind the dream. Small men dream small dreams. Mediocre men dream mediocre dreams. Great men dream great dreams. In reality you do not need to be a great man or woman in order to have great dreams. You can be at the lowest ebb of your life and still dream great dreams. In fact, the very small state of your life is the reason you need to have big dreams; it is the genesis of breaking out of that small state.

When someone criticizes you by saying your dream is impossible, it means he is a small man. Small men cannot see possibilities in impossibilities, the greatness trapped in smallness or the opportunities in problems. When you have a big dream, you should surround yourself with 'big' people. A big dreamer who surrounds himself with small men will have his dream cut to size. When your environment makes it difficult to make your dream a reality, it means that environment is too small for you. It is said that "Successful people have learned not to discuss big dreams with small minded people. Someone has said small minds talk about people, average minds talk about events, and big minds talk about vision.

The size of your dream is what will determine the size of your future. What you see in your future is what you will get in real life. Your future will rarely be bigger than your dream. Joseph's future was a great one but he saw it in his dream. Even though, no mention is made of the dreams he had as a teenager when he was working as a slave in Egypt, I believe he kept the dream in mind. As King Solomon said, *"as a man thinketh in his heart, so is he."* If your dream is small, you will have a small future and if it is big, you will have a big future.

Every part of the human body has a connection to the central nervous system. When the mind and heart decide to do something, the brain sends the message through the nerves to the appropriate part in the body to act accordingly. When you decide to pursue a dream, your brain sends a message to all parts of the body. Just as a footballer in a team sets his sights on winning a tournament, every part of his body is focused on working hard to ensure the dream is achieved. Our human body is at the beck and call of what we set our sights on. When you decide to jump, your body will ask, "how high?" As high as you want it to jump in as much as you have prepared it to do, so will it. It means when you set a small target for yourself, your body will achieve just that for you. It behooves on you to dream big so that your whole body will gravitate towards working to achieve that dream. As Brian Tracy said, *"All successful people (men and women) are big dreamers. They imagine what their future could be, ideal in every respect, and then they work every day toward their distant vision, that goal or purpose".* Whatever dream you have now, make it bigger. Think deeper, think bigger, think wider, think higher.

The Significance of a Dream Lies in the Number of Lives It Improves

God did not create you to simply survive or be a survivor. He created you to be successful, and move on to significance. Survival is the lowest level of living. When you are surviving, you merely exist. At this level, you are just focused on what will feed you, clothe you and provide you with shelter. Your life is built around meeting your basic needs. The next level is the level of success. Here, you are achieving your goals; you are able to meet more than your basic needs. At the third level, you are living a life of significance and your dreams are enabling other people to achieve their dreams. This is where your life is giving life to others and is overflowing to other people. You are not just blessed, you are a blessing! You are not just successful, you are making others successful. You are not just in right standing with God; you are helping others to be in right standing with God. Your dream gains significance when it is set on improving the lives of others.

Your Dream Creates Space for You

Dreams define the kind of person we want to be, the kind of things we want to accomplish and the kind of life we want to live generally. When your dream is sourced from God's specific purpose for your life, there is a uniqueness attached to it which can be likened to the uniqueness of your DNA. The uniqueness of your dream sets you apart from all others; it creates space for you.

There is space for everyone on this earth. I believe no matter how densely populated your town or country is, there is space for you. No matter how saturated the market place is, if your dream keeps coming back to you, there is space for you. If your dream is linked to the gift or talent God has given to you, there is space for you. No matter how successful the pioneers or players in the market place are, your dream will still create space for you. This reminds me once again about a statement made by the Brazilian author and lyricist, Paulo Coelho, "*When a person really desires something, all the universe conspires to help that person to realize his dream.*" When you start pursuing your dream, doors open, people stand up for you and things happen that would not have normally happened.

If your dream is to be a pastor, you have your congregation waiting for you. If your dream is to be a musician, you have your fans waiting to stir you up. If your dream is to be a teacher, you have your students waiting to learn from you. If your dream is to be a medical doctor, you have your patients waiting to see you. If your dream is to be an entrepreneur, your clients are waiting to patronise you. When you show up to fulfill your dream, they will also show up to play their roles. The only way people stay away from your dream is when you refuse to work out the dream.

Your Dreams Heal You

Dreams heal. The energy required to fuel your dream is both creative and restorative. The force of a dream is higher and bigger than the powers of any ailment, sickness or disease known to man. God being a dreamer knows how to aid, guide and assist you into the fulfillment of your dream without your life force being short circuited. That is why He heals you through the gravity of your dreams as His ultimate hope is that your dreams shall be fulfilled. God is not in the business of death, rather God is in the business of 'life'. Your dream will deliver you, preserve you, enrich you and nourish you - body, soul and spirit. Staying your mind on a God-inspired dream is equal to staying your mind on God and peace will be the result.

"Thou will keep him in perfect peace whose mind is stayed on thee..." Isaiah 26:3

The Dream is Not For You

God usually gives a dream to one man. But whatever dream God gives to you is not yours alone. The fact that it was given to you does not mean that it is yours. Understand therefore that even though the dream is given to you, it is not for you alone. God desires to fulfill it through you but it is not just for your sake. The main beneficiaries of the dream are the people who stand to benefit from it.

In Genesis 28:14, God told Jacob that:

"...and in you and in your seed all the families of the earth shall be blessed." Genesis 28:14b

God did not just promise to bless Jacob and his seed only but also that through him, all the families of the earth shall be blessed. As long as you continually focus on a dream that makes you a blessing to others, you will find success in life. As Mike Murdock says, *"when you make it happen for others, God will make it happen for you."* Open doors for other people and God will open doors for you. Let the focus of your dream be the betterment of others and you will continue to stay in business.

Have a Dream and Let The Dream Have You

You cannot fulfill a dream if you do not allow the dream to have you. You must first have a dream, that is, conceive it and beyond that, allow the dream to have you. In other words, it must possess you. Unless a dream consumes you, you will not have enough drive to pursue, persist and fulfill it. Before a woman becomes pregnant, she is in control of her life. She eats what she wants, walks how she wants, goes where she wants and sleeps when she wants. The moment she becomes pregnant, she gradually begins to lose some of this control over her life. If the pregnant woman refuses to make significant changes in her life for the sake of her baby, it can impact her pregnancy negatively. The change she has to make in her life is due to the demands the baby makes on her.

The point where a dream influences your life and causes you to make significant changes, is the point where we say the dream has you. When your dream has you, then it has become an obsession. Your desires, hopes and expectations must rise to a certain level of obsession if you are to realize them. Albert Einstein shared in this when he said, "I know quite certainly that I myself have no special talent; curiosity, obsession, dogged endurance, combined with self-criticism have brought me to my ideas." Einstein admits that his obsession with his work is what has contributed to his achievements. Is your dream still just a desire you are entertaining or does it consume you like fire? Do you own the dream or the dream owns you? Dreams that become a sell out are the ones which move from being owned by the dreamer to the dreamer being owned by the dream.

CHAPTER 10

THE DREAM AND THE SMALL PLACES OF LIFE

NO MATTER WHERE GOD PLACES YOU, THERE IS ALWAYS A CONNECTION BETWEEN WHERE YOU ARE AND WHERE YOU ARE DREAMING OF BEING.

n Jacob's dream of Genesis 28, the Bible gives an account of where Jacob dreamt - Genesis 28:11,

"So he came to a certain place and stayed there all night, because the sun had set. And he took one of the stones of that place and put it at his head, and he lay down in that place to sleep."

The dream Jacob had was a generational dream that contained part of the eternal purpose of God for mankind. It was also a dream that defined his life. He saw God in the dream and God spoke to Him. However, the place he was when he had the dream had no relationship with the dream he had. The nature of the place he was did not match the size of the dream. The dream was far bigger than the place he found himself in. When he woke up from the dream, he confessed that he never expected God to be in that place.

We all find ourselves in places and situations which make us doubt the possibilities in our dreams. We believe there has to be a positive correlation between our dreams and the nature of the place we find ourselves. So many people have discounted their dreams and achieved little because they were discouraged by the place in life where they found themselves. Let us embark on a journey to glean some insights from the place Jacob dreamt.

A Place of Uncertainty

The Bible describes the place Jacob dreamt from as *"a certain place."* The place had no name, no fixed address. It was just a certain place in between where he was coming from and where he was going to. Jacob had just started life independent of his parents. He was going to a place he was not familiar with and not sure of how things will turn out. He had left all his father's wealth behind and in material terms, had nothing on him. It represents a place in your life where you are uncertain of what the future holds for you. You wonder whether it was a wise decision to have taken a particular risk in pursuing your dream. This can be when you have had to leave the comfort of your parent's home, country or a secured job towards the future you believe in, or perhaps, you work outside a familiar environment or have started your own company.

In this uncertain place in life, you have a destination in mind but you still have occasional doubts if everything is going to be alright. God spoke to Jacob assuring him of how certain his future was and referred to His (God) fulfilled purpose in the life of Abraham (his grandfather) and Isaac (his father). When you are uncertain of your future that is when you need to focus on the dream you have always cherished. This is when the telescopic function of dreams comes into play. You must bring the dream into remembrance and focus on it. Do not focus on the uncertainty of the dream; focus on the promise of the dream. Remember, it is better to be on the journey to fulfilling a dream and be found in an uncertain place than to live without a dream and be found in a place of uncertainty. For the former, at least you know you are still on the path of accomplishing your dream.

A Place of Darkness

When Jacob arrived at the "uncertain place" it was sunset and so we are told *"...he stayed there all night..."* The small places of life are also places of darkness. It was the night season of his life. This is the son of a wealthy man having to sleep at a place where he could not even light a fire to keep him warm. Night denotes a season of darkness. It represents the season in your life when you cannot see your way clearly; you just cannot find your way around. It is also the season when you are susceptible to the enemy's attacks. During the dark season, you do not see anyone else so you are usually lonely and the realities of life hit you hard.

In that season of susceptibility, the source of the dream gave Him assurance of divine protection. He saw some glimmering light in the midst of darkness. He saw some light at the end of the dark tunnel. He saw the silver lining in the dark clouds.

A Place of Discomfort

Apart from the darkness in that place, it was also a place of discomfort according to Genesis 28:11 *"And he took one of the stones of that place and put it at his head, and he lay down in that place to sleep."*

A place in life where you have to use a stone as a pillow is a hard and uncomfortable place to be. During this season, you find it difficult to get results and every form of comfort you enjoyed is taken away from you. It could be the loss of your car, house, position or money. But it is when you are in a small, hard and uncomfortable place in life that you have to dream big to take yourself out of that situation.

The nature and size of your environment and season should not determine the size of your dream. Learn to dream big even when you are in small, hard and uncomfortable situations in life. The alternative of not dreaming at all is to remain in that situation forever. Remember that a season of discomfort precedes a lifetime of comfort. Within every discomfort you are facing today, there is some comfort waiting to emerge tomorrow.

A Place of Small Resources

Jacob's father Isaac was a rich man but Jacob left his father's house with just a staff and some oil. His situation was so dire that "...*he took one of the stones of that place and put it at his head, and he lay down in that place to sleep* (Genesis 28:11b)". It represents a place of little or no resources for realizing your dream.

Resources are usually one of the main constraints to achieving dreams. I believe that you need to first have a dream/vision before you attract the provision you need to fulfill it. Vision always attracts provision no matter how big the provision is. An analysis of 'Provision' reveals a lot - 'pro' means in 'support of' so 'provision' means 'in support of vision.' It presupposes that you must have the vision first and what you need in support of the vision will come. When you take up the responsibility your dreams impose on you, it will attract the necessary resources you need.

The only resource needed to dream big is your imagination. You do not need to employ all your wits, you only need your imagination faculty alive. Dreaming big is about tapping into the powers of your imagination. The fact that you have small resources does not mean you cannot dream big. The size of your dream should not be based on the availability or quantum of resources you have. The dream is usually bigger than the resources available.

When the dream is smaller than the resources available, you are not stretching enough to give your best. And when you do not stretch yourself, you never know how far you can go so you operate below your full potential. When Jacob received the dream of his future, all he had on him was a staff and a bottle of oil. If even he had any spare clothes with him, it was not enough for him to use as a pillow so he had to use a stone instead. That was how under-resourced he was.

When Bill Gates was dreaming of a personal computer on the desk of every home, he was operating from a garage. When Michael Dell was dreaming of Dell computers, he was operating from a college dormitory. If you want to move from lack to abundance, you must first dream big. Big dreams attract abundance; small dreams attract small resources.

A Place of Sleep

The small places of life are also places of sleep. What was Jacob doing in this "certain place?" Genesis 28:11 gives us the answer, *"...and he lay down in that place to sleep."* What else can you do in the night season of life other than to fall asleep and await the break of day? The place of sleep represent the season when your life is in shut down mode. Here, there is not much activity, it is a down time and you are not making conspicuous and significant progress in life.

Sleep in the Bible is not always good. In King Solomon's time, the stealing of a prostitute's baby occurred at night. In Jesus' parable of the weeds, after the farmer sowed good seeds in his field, the one who sowed weeds did so at night when he slept. When you fall asleep in life, the enemy sneaks in to take advantage. However, you may find yourself in a certain place where there is little you can do but simply sleep like Jacob did. Jacob was on a journey to a faraway place and on the way, he became tired and it was getting late so he had to sleep. Can you fault him in such a situation? The conditions facing him put him to sleep.

When you start a business and after much effort you are still not getting a lot of clients, it can put your business to sleep. When you are expecting something and you have done all you need to do but you still have not obtained the results you need, you are inclined to simply wait and that puts you to sleep. When you are in a situation that requires divine intervention from God, you simply can do nothing but wait on God and that is similar to being in sleep mode. Life can make you so weary that you just want to put everything on hold and simply do nothing.

When Jacob went to sleep in an unknown and therefore possibly dangerous place, God did not allow the enemy to take advantage of him. God was awake in his life when he was asleep. When you have a relationship with God, He watches over your life when you go to sleep. Your life may slow down and you feel nothing is happening but God could still be working on you during those moments of silence and inactivity. You do not have to always hear noise or see movement to know productivity is taking place somewhere. There can be silence and still something is happening. As I write this book, you will hear the noise of my typing regularly but there are also times when I pause and you hear nothing. When I pause, I am meditating and it is out of the meditation that I get more insight to share with you. In the same vein, when God is silent and your life is in sleep mode, God may still be doing something productive in your life unknowingly. During the season of sleep, do not put your dreams to sleep, keep your hopes alive.

A Place of Small Achievements

The small place of life can also be when your achievement level is too small compared to the size of the dream you want to achieve. When God told Jacob that his descendants will be as the dust of the earth, he did not have a fiancée.

He promised him blessing when he was unemployed. When Joseph dreamt of being a great leader, he was not a leader in his house and he had not earned the respect of his brothers, yet he dreamt big.

The size of your dream should not be informed by the size of your past or current achievements. The society usually refers to your past to determine what you can do in future. God does not consult your past to design your future; He knows your future from the beginning. If past experience was the criteria for God to implant big dreams in hearts, then David would not have qualified to be a king seeing he began as a mere shepherd.

You do not need to be a big achiever to dream big; rather, your dreams will inspire you to break out of the mold of small thinking into the arena of big achievements. Your dreams define your achievements, whilst your achievements glorify your dreams. Today, you may not have your own musical album but you can dream of being an international gospel artiste. You may not have started a business before but you can dream of being an international business executive. You may be struggling with being stable in the faith but you can dream of being used greatly by God across the globe.

An Unconducive Environment

The environment you find yourself in can also be a small

place in fulfilling your dreams. However, it should not determine the size of your dream. If you have ever been to Dubai, you will agree with me that it is one of the most amazing and modern cities in the world today. It has become a global city, a business hub and is the twenty second most expensive city in the world, surpassing London. It is also the most expensive city in the Middle East. But did you know that Dubai is located right in the sandy Arabian Desert? With a hot desert climate, a day in Dubai is usually sunny and humid making life a bit uncomfortable.

But in that desert you will find the first indoor ski resort in the Middle East with an actual snow experience throughout the year. The world's first underwater hotel, the Hydropolis is found in Dubai. The city also features the eighth wonder of the world - modern cities built in the shape of a palm tree with a trunk. These are just a few of some of the wonders of Dubai.

They have been able to achieve all this because they have refused to allow their dreams to be defined by their environment. They have dreamt big in spite of their hostile environment and created an oasis in a desert. Their dreams and commitment have transformed a desert into a fruitful land. If you find yourself in a family, church, organization or community that is barren, dry, unproductive, poor and stagnating, do not let that define your dreams.

God can cause your environment to suite you. He will

make your environment fertile and productive because of you! He will give you something of value that will attract affluent merchants, wise men and kings to you! Never move from where God has planted you. When you stay where God plants you, He takes care of you; when you stay where He has not asked you to stay, you take care of yourself. If He instructs you to go through the wilderness, He will provide you with manna from Heaven, water from the rock and cool temperatures with His cloud. Do not change your dream because of the environment; rather change your environment through the power of dreams.

A Place of Small Preparation

A small place can also be when you are at a place where your preparation is inadequate to achieve your dreams. Performance is a function of your preparation. The quality of your preparation determines the quality of your performance. Whatever you want to achieve in life, you must prepare for it. As the common saying goes, *"when you fail to prepare, you prepare to fail."*

However, you do not have to wait to be 101% prepared before you dream. Dreaming big does not require preparation but after dreaming big, you have to prepare yourself to fulfill it. Your big dreams will drive you to prepare well. Whenever God calls and implants a dream in the heart of a person, the person is usually not fully prepared but God still gives him the dream. God does not call only the prepared but He prepares the called. When Joseph dreamt of being a great leader, he was a pampered young boy in his father's house. He was the least prepared to be a great leader but God still gave him the dream. When Oprah Winfrey told her father that in future "she wants to talk and be paid for it", she was just a 12-year old girl staying with her parents and did not have the kind of skills that will enable her to earn money from speaking. Yet, she did not allow that to prevent her from dreaming big.

You are free to dream of being an international business executive even when you are still a student. You can envision managing a large investment firm when you are struggling with your personal finances. Though you are not well prepared for the dream, the dream will spur you on to prepare for it.

A place of youthfulness or ageing

Another small place in relation to dreams is our age – it is either we think we are too young or too old to dream and achieve big dreams. Some believe they are too young or too old to marry, to start their own business, to become the CEO of the company they work in, to be promoted or to build their own house.

Joseph and David were all young when they dreamt of their future, and as young adults, they started working towards their dreams. Also, what comes to mind when you hear of KFC? Chicken of course! They promise serving the "world's best tasting chicken with home styled sides and freshly made chicken sandwiches." They have been in business for 60 years with over 15000 outlets in 105 countries and territories around the world. Unlike most of America's strong brands which were started by young people, KFC was founded by a sixty five year-old called Colonel Sanders. Colonel Sanders did not allow growing older to become an excuse to the pursuit of the dream in his heart.

He may not have known about Caleb in the Bible but he had the spirit of Caleb. In Joshua 14:6-15, Caleb reminded Joshua of God's promise after spying on the land of Canaan. Caleb believed that Just as just as you are never too young to experience God's promises for your life, you are also never too old to experience His promises. Never allow age to erase the memory of what God has inspired in you. In spite of being eighty five years, he kept Joshua in remembrance of God's destiny for them. The promises of God are no respecter of age but faith. If you are eighty years and you have not experienced God's promise for your life, it is not too late to claim it.

If it's about being all that God created you to be and accomplishing what He brought you on earth to do, then age is not an issue; it's your availability that matters. God needs your availability more than your ability. When you make yourself available, He will increase your ability to perform, notwithstanding age.

The 20th and 21st centuries have brought down the barriers that age poses to living a life that is fulfilled and full of impact. Take a cursory look at the business leaders in your country today and backtrack to when they started business; they all started when they were young. Richard Branson started his first business venture at the age of sixteen. Bill Gates started Microsoft at twenty years old. Facebook was started by another twenty year old, Mark Zuckerberg. So are you going to allow age to still be an excuse for not pursuing your dream?

A Place of Inadequacy

You are in a small place when you consider yourself too small for the dream. Moses found himself in such a place when God called him and gave him a dream. The first question he asked God was "...who am I that I should go to Pharaoh, and that I should bring the children of Israel out of Egypt?" (Exodus 3:11). Whenever you question yourself in relation to a dream, it reveals a feeling of inadequacy. It is when you think you are so small and the dream seems too big for you.

When a dream is conceived, it is always bigger than the person; that is the nature of every dream. It is therefore no news that you think the dream is bigger than you. In fact, if you want to grow and progress in life, you must always have dreams that are bigger than you. Stud Tekel writes that *"most of us have dreams that are too small for our spirits."* Your dream must be bigger than you so it will stretch your potential. This is what some people do not also understand about leaders - they always have dreams which are bigger than them. They would not be leaders without those big dreams.

Do not be like the brothers of Joseph who doubted his ability to fulfill his dreams. Understand that the dream will not happen in a day but over a period of time, so you will have time to grow yourself to achieve the dream. When your dreams are smaller than you, you retrogress in life. When they are bigger than you, it brings advancement in life.

A Place of Disability or Inability

Disability and inability can also be a small place. Let me share with you the story of one young man who found himself in such a small place but has managed to break out of it. At the age of seventeen, he beat the existing 100m Paralympics record with a time of 11.72 seconds during a school race. A few months after, he won gold at the Athens Paralympics breaking the world record. He also won the bronze medal in the 100m event. At the age of twenty one (in 2008), he won three gold medals at the Paralympics games. He was the first athlete in history to win gold in

100m, 200m and 400m in his category in the Paralympics games. Four years later, he won two gold medals and a bronze medal in the 2012 London Paralympics games. Oscar Pistorius is the first Paralympics athlete to win a World Championship medal.

But guess what? South African born Oscar had both legs amputated below the knee and replaced with prosthetic legs before he learnt how to walk. Growing up, his first excuse could have been that he was physically incapable and disabled. Also, he could have played the blame game and blamed God, his parents and the hospital for his state. He could have pitied himself when other kids picked on him because he was not a 'normal' child but he did not. He took charge of his destiny with family support and has become a successful sportsman.

Excuses exclude you from fulfilling your dream. God chooses you despite your numerous excuses. That is why God was surprised at the many excuses Moses was giving when He gave him a dream. Moses felt God could not use him because he was slow of speech but God had a solution for it. When you are connected to the manufacturer, there's no spare part that you cannot get. For every excuse, God has an antidote.

The greatest disability is not physical but mental. Mental disability is more powerful than physical disability. Excuses create mental disability. So what's your excuse for not pursuing your dreams? You stammer? Too short?

Too tall? Too big? Too small? Physically challenged? God gave Moses, Aaron. Pistorius was given artificial legs. Whatever you lack, God has. Within every disability there's, an ability; efficiency in every deficiency and advantage in every disadvantage. The disability or inability should not disable your dreams.

A Big God in Small Places

In our key passage, when Jacob woke up from the destiny shaping dream, this is what he said according to Genesis 28:11b, "...*Surely the LORD is in this place, and I did not know it.*" Jacob knew that the kind of place he was in was a small place that's why he said God was in there and he did not know it. He also did not expect God to be in such places and this perception is held by so many other Christians. Many people believe that God is only found in only deeply spiritual, holy, comfortable, big and beautiful places. So such an unspiritual, small, hard, uncomfortable and ugly place will not be blessed with the presence of God.

But as Jacob's experience reveals, God is not found only in the beautiful, sophisticated places and situations of life. The presence of lack, smallness, hardness and discomfort does not mean God is absent. He can be found in the most obscure and hard places of life. He can be present but you will be ignorant of it. The fact that you cannot sense the presence of God now does not mean He is not there. It is not because of the place that God is present; but because of the person. You can be down in life and God will be up in your life. You may feel small and God will see you big. You can have small thoughts about yourself yet God still has great thoughts about you.

CHAPTER 11

INTERPRETING DREAMS

ANY TIME YOU OPEN YOUR MIND TO A
REVELATION OR DREAM, YOU HAVE OPENED
SOMEONE'S WORLD.

The ability to interpret dreams was very important in Old Testament times. Great kings like Nebuchadnezzar and Pharaoh had officials such as magicians and wise men whose functions included interpreting dreams. It was so important that at a point, King Nebuchadnezzar threatened to kill his wise men if they do not give him an interpretation of a puzzling dream. In fact, he demanded that he be reminded of the dream itself because he had forgotten it.

Dreaming is different from interpreting the dream. It is not enough to be a dreamer; you must develop the ability to interpret dreams. A dream is useless without the ability to interpret it. Interpreting the dream is the meaning you attach to the dream; it is your explanation or point of view. It is your understanding of the dream: its scope, requirements and positioning required to fulfill it. The interpretation process demands how the dream fits into a larger purpose, who the key actors are, accepting those key actors and knowing what to do to translate the dream into reality.

It is not every dreamer that knows how to interpret a dream. There are many people with dreams that are not doing anything about it because they do not know what to do. Some want to be worship leaders but they do not know the steps to take on a daily basis to draw them closer to their dream. Others want to be international business executives but they do not know how to start from where they are. When Joseph was in prison according to Genesis 40, his new prison colleagues, Pharaoh's wine server and baker both had dreams in the same night but they did not have the ability to interpret them which made them sad. Pharaoh was also greatly disturbed at a point because he had dreamt and could not interpret it. Let me share with you more on what interpreters of dreams do.

Dream Interpreters Provide Solutions to Human Enigmas or Complex Problems

The best examples of dream interpreters in the Bible, Daniel and Joseph, both worked as senior government officials by applying their dream interpreting abilities. They ascended to high levels of influence by virtue of solving complex problems and when they took up their new positions, they continued to solve complex problems. They solved problems which neither their bosses nor officials who were employed to solve these problems could solve.

Dream interpreters are problem solvers who specialize in providing solutions to human enigmas. They solve problems at all levels – personal, organizational and national. Joseph solved the problem of fellow prison mates. The prison warden might have noticed this trait which is why he made him a leader over his prison mates (apart from the favor of God upon him). What distinguishes dream interpreters from all others is the grace they have to solve problems others cannot solve.

When Joseph was called in to interpret Pharaoh's dream, all the wise men and magicians of Pharaoh had failed at interpreting it. Dream interpreters provide answers to questions that others cannot provide and prescribe solutions to puzzling problems. They fix what others cannot fix. I believe that this is the level God would want believers to operate in. It is included in our being the light of the world and salt of the earth. Every dream interpreter does not just give meaning to a dream but also provide wise solutions to the enigmas associated with the dream.

There are so many problems facing the world today –

conflicts, youth delinquency, drug addictions, HIV AIDS and teenage pregnancy to mention a few. The world is still reeling under the weight of these challenges and they want better solutions. Though you may not provide all the solutions, there is grace available to handle each of them and you have one at least one portion of such grace upon your life.

You need dream interpreters to help you fulfill your dream. However, God can also give you the grace to interpret dreams. In fact, no matter the work you do, you need to pray to God for that grace and also personally strive to be a dream interpreter. Your personal value shoots up when you are recognized as the go-to person when someone is faced with a puzzling problem. It is only when you provide solutions other people cannot provide that you get rewards other people do not get. You must get to the level where Kings and Queens will flock to you for solutions to problems they cannot solve because they know you have the divine grace to solve puzzles.

Everyone is a dream interpreter for someone. In other words, everyone is called to provide solutions to someone which hardly anyone else can offer. We are all endowed with different abilities which if we stretch ourselves and develop, will make us unique solution providers. The fulfillment of your dream must provide solutions and answers to other people. Your dream must solve problems and answer questions and not create more problems and raise more questions. It must also feed into solving the problems of other people.

God Gives The Ability to Interpret Dreams

The ability to interpret dreams comes from God according to Genesis 40:8,

"...And Joseph said to them, Do not interpretations belong to God? Tell me your dreams, I pray you."

The wisdom to comprehend what to do about the dream is from God not man. If you do not know what to do about a dream or an idea, ask God to give you the understanding to know what to do. He also gifts people with the spirit of wisdom, knowledge and counsel to guide people in fulfilling their dreams; but the ultimate source of this ability is God.

However, every dream interpreter in the Bible went through some kind of training which is utilized in the process of interpreting dreams. Daniel went through three years of training to serve before Nebuchadnezzar. Joseph also went through a lot of on-the-job training before he became a Prime Minister in Egypt.

Interpreting Dreams is the Ability to Connect the Dots

When God communicates through dreams at night, He does so through symbols at times. A typical example is the dream Pharaoh had as narrated in Genesis 41. In his dream, he saw a river, seven fat looking cows and seven ugly and lean looking cows. Then he also saw that the lean and ugly cows ate up the fat cows. His second dream was also full of symbols. The dreams were not straightforward or clear; it was encoded so required decoding to understand it.

What Pharaoh needed was someone to interpret what the river, the fat cows, the lean cows and the fat cows eating up the lean cows represented and what should be done. This act of giving meanings and drawing relationships between the things he saw in his dream is what I call connecting the dots. Whenever you conceive a dream, it is initially not so clear and understandable. Dreams are conceived in bits and pieces. God does not reveal everything to us at the beginning; He rather reveals a part of His desire for us and as we pursue it, it gradually unfolds before us.

Dream interpretation is the ability to give meaning to the dream by connecting one aspect of the dream to another. It is having a thorough understanding of the meaning of the dream. It enables you to connect seemingly unrelated aspects of the dreams to one another to create a big picture. It shows you the big picture and reveals the brush and color of paint to apply and the kind of shapes needed to paint it.

Interpreting Dreams Entails Understanding the Times You Live In

Whenever God implants a dream in the heart of a person, that dream is a part of a larger plan God is working out. Your dream is not isolated; it is connected to another person's dream and they all work together to achieve an eternal purpose of God. In interpreting a dream, you must understand the times you live in and find out how it fits into that larger purpose and plan of God.

It was said of David in Acts 13:36,

"For David, after he had served God's will and purpose and counsel in his own generation, fell asleep (died) and was buried among his forefathers..."

David fulfilled God's purpose in his own generation. This implies his purpose was for his generation. If he had lived in another generation, he may not have been able to fulfill it.

There is a relationship between your dream and the times you live in. The dream must be relevant to those times. When a dream is pursued in the right time, it strikes a chord with the people and the impact is huge.

The sons of Issachar were described as a people who understood the times according to 1 Chronicles 12:32,

"Of the sons of Issachar who had understanding of the times, to know what Israel ought to do, their chiefs were two

hundred; and all their brethren were at their command."

The tribe of Issachar had the ability to understand the times or recognize seasons they were in. The Bible found this worth mentioning because it was an important ability to possess. The ability to understand the times enabled them to know what Israel should do. When you know the season you are in, you will know what to do. It also means that what you do should be a function of the season you are in. When you do the right thing at the right time, you get maximum results.

Find out what God is doing in your time, in your nation or community and ascertain how your dream fits into it. Study the trends of your career, industry or market in which your dream places you. Be abreast with the history, key success factors and future of that industry. For instance, in planning your career in this century, you need to understand that we are in an era of globalization and advancement in information and communication technology. This means you need to think global, learn how ICT can be applied to your work and develop the ICT skills you need to excel.

The Interpretation of Dreams Creates Passion Which Works For or Against The Journey to Fulfilling The Dream.

In Genesis 40:7, Joseph *"... asked Pharaoh's officers who were with him in the custody of his lord's house, saying, 'why do you look so sad today? And they said to him, we each have had a dream, and there is no interpreter of it."* They had dreamt but could not interpret it and this made them sad. When Pharaoh also dreamt and could not interpret it himself, *"his spirit was troubled"* according to Genesis 41:8. Just as the absence of an interpreter made them sad, when it was interpreted to them and they found it favorable, it released an emotion of happiness in them. Sadness and happiness are both emotions which influence the pursuit of our dreams.

Passion is fuel for every dream. It supplies the energy, drive and enthusiasm that keep you going in pursuit of a dream. It is difficult to fulfill a dream without passion because the journey can be torturous. Listen to what the late Steve Jobs of Apple Computers said, *"It's hard to tell with these Internet startups if they're really interested in building companies or if they're just interested in the money. I can tell you, though; If they don't really want to build a company, they won't luck into it. That's because it's so hard that if you don't have a passion, you'll give up."* Steve Jobs says that if you are an internet startup and you do not have passion you will give up because it's hard to survive and build a successful internet startup company. This applies to everything you want to build in life.

Attitude or Character Determines The Response to The Interpretation of Dreams

In other words, what you get out of a dream is determined by your character. You will never get more out of a dream than your character will allow you to. In effect, two people may have or hear the same dream but their responses will be different due to differences in character. Character is the differentiator.

For instance, when Joseph shared his dream with his family, it generated different responses. They all interpreted and understood the dream to mean Joseph was going to be a great leader in future and they will have to submit to his leadership at a point. However, his brothers envied and hated him in spite of their interpretation of the dream. His father Jacob initially was skeptical but the Bible tells us he finally decided to keep this prophetic revelation in mind.

The brothers of Joseph did not have the character to contain the dream of their brother. Instead of being happy for their brother, they were envious, jealous and it rose to hatred. And the hatred was strong enough to make them want to kill him. If they were not his brothers and he was not a man of character when he became Prime Minister in Egypt, he could have killed them or thrown them in jail. Your benefit from the dream of others is influenced a lot by your character.

Every dream requires a certain character to realize it. In a lot of circumstances, at the point of dreaming, you may not have the character required to make it a reality. That is one reason the dream is not fulfilled immediately you dreamt it. The dreamer will have to be worked on through a process to develop the right character. Character influences the survival and sustainability of a dream.

CHAPTER 12

PROPHESYING TO YOUR DREAM

PROPHECY IS PAINTING THE PICTURE OF YOUR TOMORROW

The road to fulfilling your God-given dream is not always straight. Neither is it always a highway. It may be rough and bumpy with sharp curves seemingly leading to nowhere. Every dream goes through several stages before its fulfillment. The fulfillment of a dream may not happen immediately after conception.

There will be a time you will have to negotiate several curves, meander your way through a maze-like route giving the impression you do not know where you are going. At another time, you will just be "plateauing". At this stage you will feel like you are not making any progress with your life because you are neither moving forward or backwards.

Before you get to the mountain top every dreamer desires to be, you will go down a steep, unfriendly and seemingly never-ending slope. And as you know, every steep slope sends you into either a valley or the foot of a higher ground. The valley could be your lowest ebb in the pursuit of your dream. God teaches more about this through the Prophet Ezekiel.

In Ezekiel chapter 37, Prophet Ezekiel was transported to a valley by the Spirit. The valley was full of many dry human bones. God later told the prophet that the bones represented the people of Israel.

"Then He said to me, 'Son of man, these bones are the whole house of Israel. They indeed say, our bones are dry, our hope is lost, and we ourselves are cut off!" Ezekiel 37:11

Take note that the bones were human bones and they were dry and many. Secondly, God told him it was representative of people who say their hope is lost and they are cut off in life. In the third chapter of this book, I stated that dreams are the things we hope for. Therefore, our hopes can also be our dreams. In effect, when a person says his "hope is lost", he is also saying his "dreams are lost." It is therefore right for me to say that a person who believes his dreams are lost and that he has no hope in life can be likened to dry bones in a valley.

When you slide down in life to the point where you lose sight of your dream and give up on it, your life is dismembered, disorganized and looks useless. Like the dry bones, you lack form, structure, direction, strength and most importantly, the drive to live. A man without hope (without a dream for that matter) is at the lowest ebb of his life. Without a dream, you are merely existing and not living.

With this understanding, let us read more of this account in Ezekiel 37: 1-14

"The hand of the LORD came upon me and brought me out in the Spirit of the LORD, and set me down in the midst of the valley; and it was full of bones.

"Then He caused me to pass by them all around, and behold, there were very many in the open valley; and indeed they were very dry.

And He said to me, "Son of man, can these bones live?" So I answered, 'O Lord GOD, You know.'

Again He said to me, "Prophesy to these bones, and say to them, "O dry bones, hear the word of the LORD!"

"Thus says the Lord GOD to these bones: "Surely I will cause breath to enter into you, and you shall live."

"I will put sinews on you and bring flesh upon you; and you shall live. Then you shall know that I am the LORD."

So I prophesied as I was commanded; and as I prophesied, there was a noise, and suddenly a rattling; and the bones came together, bone to bone.

Indeed, as I looked, the sinews and the flesh came upon them, and the skin covered them over; but there was no breath in them.

Also He said to me, "Prophesy to the breath, prophesy, son of man, and say to the breath, "Thus says the Lord GOD: "Come from the four winds, O breath, and breathe on these slain, that they may live."

So I prophesied as He commanded me, and breath came into them, and they lived, and stood upon their feet, an exceedingly great army.

Then He said to me, "Son of man, these bones are the whole house of Israel. They indeed say, our bones are dry, our hope is lost, and we ourselves are cut off!"

"Therefore prophesy and say to them, "thus says the Lord GOD: behold O My people, I will open your graves and cause you to come up from your graves, and bring you into the land of Israel.

"Then you shall know that I am the LORD, when I have opened your graves, O My people, and brought you up from your graves.

"I will put My Spirit in you, and you shall live, and I will place you in your own land. Then you shall know that I, the LORD, have spoken it and performed it, says the LORD."

When The Dream Lacks the Life of God

In verse 7 and 8, the bones came together and they developed flesh. But the process was not complete because "there was no breath in them." The coming together of the bones and the development of the sinews and flesh gave it form, structure and appeal. They were close to being alive but they were not alive because there was no breath in them. Keep in mind that the dry bones represent the people who believe they have lost their hope and have no dream to live for.

After Prophet Ezekiel prophesied to the bones, they started coming together. The people who were dismembered, scattered and had lost their sense of purpose and value in life received a restoration of hope. It means they started to have a glimmer of hope and then the dream began to take shape. The various parts of the dream connected one to another. It started taking shape so you could tell what it was really about. However, it had no breath or life in it so it was still far from being a dream that could make impact. This means it is possible for a dream to have form and structure yet because it is not alive, it is unable to make impact.

The twelve disciples went through this experience. After the death of Jesus and through to His resurrection, all the dreams the disciples had were put on the backburner. This is evident when Peter said he was going back to fishing and the other disciples joined him. They had not forgotten about the dream but it was in the background. They lost hope in those dreams, were confused, lived in fear and lost their sense of purpose. The pain, disappointment and discouragement from the death of Jesus had overshadowed the pursuit of their dreams when Jesus was alive.

When a dream lacks the breath of God, it may be beautifully written on paper but it is unable to leave the paper and manifest in real life. You may have laid it out beautifully in a business plan but it remains just that – a plan. You may have pursued an educational program so you will be equipped to accomplish it but you graduate and find some other work to do rather than pursue it. It is akin to a car that cannot be driven; an airplane that cannot fly; a train that cannot move. It is not dead but it is as good as dead.

The lives of some people are grounded not because they do not have all the resources they need but because they lack the spiritual impetus to kick start their dream. If the dream is from God, you will need the breath of God to give it life. When God created Adam, there was no life in him and so he was as good as dead till God breathed His life into him. The life of God is what gives life to every dream that is from God. No God-given dream flies without the life of God.

When The Dream Gets The Life of God

God commanded Ezekiel to prophesy to the "breath" (from the four winds) to enter the bodies so that they will live. When he did, this is what happened:

"So I prophesied as He commanded me, and breath came into them, and they lived, and stood upon their feet, an exceedingly great army." Ezekiel 37:10

When Ezekiel prophesied, breath (which represents the life of God) entered them. Every dream without the participation of God is a dead dream. It may look lively and alive but it still lacks the real life of God. It may look durable, beautiful and magnificent but it is just a matter of time and the storms of life will blow it away.

Furthermore, "they lived, stood upon their feet and was a great army." Before then, they were dead, lay down motionless and were not considered even an army. When life enters your dream, it can fly; it can take you to places you never dreamed possible. It gets strength to move and be active. It is put in motion to achieve its purpose. It brings meaning and progress to your life. The life of God will put you in pole position as your dream is activated. It strengthens you and you are able to withstand the storms of life that will come against you.

The Delivery from the Four Winds of God

*"Then said he unto me, "Prophesy unto the wind, prophesy, son of man, and say unto the wind, thus saith the Lord God; Come from **the four winds**, O breath and breathe upon these slain, that they may live."* Ezekiel 37:9

The mysterious concept of the four winds introduces to us a realm or dimension of prophetic authority uncommon to man.

This is the realm of prophetic authority that employs instruments that God has already set in place through His word but which are still not easily accessible because of the lack of prophetic insight by the church.

It is God's will for us to employ the mysterious four winds of Heaven for creative miracles and wonders, fruitfulness and fertility, favour and flavour, speedy vengeance and judgement upon our enemies.

When we employ these instruments of God, we receive amazing results. Sometimes we get stuck, even in our prayers because we have not employed the instrument required to effectively tackle the situation!

God Means Business With These Four Winds.

God has weapons in His armoury! For example, The Word of God, Arrows of God, Fire of God, Blood of Jesus to mention but just a few. The Four Winds are also weapons! Read my new book, "The Mystery of the Four Winds of God."

These winds of God will bring back missing and vital ingredients to the success and survival of your dream.

Prophetic Painting of Your Dream

What brought the dry and scattered bones together was when Ezekiel spoke the prophetic word from God to the bones. After, they came together but lay motionless with no life in them, till God again instructed him to command the four winds from the four corners of the earth to enter them. In all cases, Ezekiel was given words to speak; he spoke what God told him to say. Ezekiel did not speak his own words; he spoke the word of God.

He spoke what he heard God speak to him over the situation and an army was raised out of the valley of dry bones. The words he spoke were not ordinary words but prophetic words; words inspired by the Holy Spirit. An inspired word from God concerning His dream for you is capable of resurrecting your dead dream.

When God speaks concerning your future, He uses a lot of imagery. At one time, He told Abraham, "And I will make thy seed as the dust of the earth: so that if a man can number the dust of the earth, then shall thy seed also be numbered" (Genesis 13:16). He also told Moses about the deliverance of the Israelites from Egypt, "And I am come down to deliver them out of the hand of the Egyptians, and to bring them up out of that land unto a good land a large, unto a land flowing with milk and honey..." (Exodus 3:8).

These words painted a mental picture of the future for the recipients. When God gave words to Ezekiel to prophesy, they were specific words which painted a picture of what is to be done for the army of people to rise. Prophecy paints pictures of our tomorrow. When God speaks concerning the future of a person, He paints a picture of the future of that person. We can do same when we speak God's words in relation to our dreams. That is what we need to do to have the life of God quicken every dream God has given us.

Speak to the dream the very words you heard God speak to you when He gave you the dream. Even if He spoke through another person to you, speak those words that the person spoke. Use the exact words God used. Alternatively, speak what you want to happen in relation to your dream. Ezekiel wanted the bones to connect, one to the other and that is just what he spoke. When He wanted breath to enter them and give them life, he spoke exactly that.

For persons who are yet to receive a word from God concerning their future, wait on the Lord and hear Him speak into your spirit. Speak those words to yourself continually. Locate yourself in the written Word of God and speak the words God highlights in your heart concerning your future and your dream.

As you prophesy, the various things that are needed to make the dream work come together. As you imagine and confess, you literally psyche yourself up spiritually to also make it happen. Remember what God told Joshua after the death of Moses:

"This book of the law shall not depart out of thy mouth; but thou shalt meditate therein day and night; that thou mayest observe to do according to all that is written therein: for then thou shalt make thy way prosperous, and then thou shalt have good success." Joshua 1:8

The first part *"shall not depart out of thy mouth"* implies it shall always be on your lips and that refers to confession, which is the same as prophetic declarations. The final part of this verse says when you do all that is written therein, then you will prosper and experience success. Therefore the prophetic painting of your dream is a key to walking in the future designed for you by God.

The Economic Prophets - Who are they?

Let me share an analogy with you. In the world of technology, there are some experts who are referred to as economic prophets. They are not prophets as we find in the church but they are prophets of the future of technology. Others refer to them as futurists and some are found in places like Silicon Valley. They study trends, patterns and predict what will happen in future. They talk about challenges that will emerge and proffer how technology can overcome these challenges.

The words of these futurists are held in high esteem; ground breaking ideas drip from them. Some companies employ such people to work for them and all they do is predict the future and advise them on what they should do. They are similar to the sons of Isacchar who the Bible said *"which were men that had understanding of the times and knew what Israel ought to do...and all their brethren were at their commandment"* (1 Chronicles 12:32).

There are technology companies that clamour to have audience with these people. When they speak, their words are clung on to like the Bible. Software developers and programmers deconstruct what they say and try to make something out of it. New technologies and inventions have emerged from their prophetic statements. Through the power of imagination and skill, people including scientists go to work to maximize the ideas of these prophets.

CHAPTER 13

DEALING WITH DREAM KILLERS

YOU NEVER KNOW WHO'S LOOKING TO KILL YOU
UNTIL THEY START KILLING YOUR DREAM.

In most situations, when God gives someone a dream or you conceive a dream, the threats or challenges to the dream is conspicuously absent from it. At this stage of conception, what we see is the end of the dream not the process; the glorious part not the story behind it; the destination and not the path. When you ask a child what he will want to achieve in future or become, he will paint a beautiful picture of the future devoid of the challenges associated with it. That is how we all dream. It is normal human behavior.

Joseph will tell you that when he dreamt as recounted in Genesis 37:5-9, he never saw threats or enemies in it:

"Now Joseph had a dream, and he told it to his brothers; and they hated him even more.

So he said to them, "Please hear this dream which I have dreamed:

"There we were, binding sheaves in the field. Then behold, my sheaf arose and also stood upright; and indeed your sheaves stood all around and bowed down to my sheaf."

Then he dreamed still another dream and told it to his brothers, and said, "Look, I have dreamed another dream. And this time, the sun, the moon, and the eleven stars bowed down to me."

In his first dream, his sheaf rose and the sheaves of his brothers bowed to his. There is no account of an attempt by the sheaves of his brothers to burn or destroy his sheaf. In the second dream also, he saw part of the solar system bowing to him; there was no mention of the sun trying to burn him or stars falling on him.

A critical study of dreams in the Bible reveals that God does not reveal the full picture of His dream for a person all at once. He does not show you everything about the dream; there are certain details that are totally absent. Critical amongst what He does not reveal is the issue of the challenges and threats to you and your dream. I call these threats dream killers.

Mike Murdock wrote that "God does not reveal to you what you will go through, He only shows you where He is taking you to". God does not reveal all the dream killers you will have to face in the process of achieving your dream. As a result, there are many people who think once it is God who gave them the dream, they will not face any giants on the way.

It is idealistic to think you have no dream killers but that ideal does not exist in this world. In fact, even in the most perfect world which is Heaven, the enemy tries to thwart their dreams. When Joseph told his family about his dreams, he was being naïve. He thought that as his family, they should be happy for him. He thought the world was a perfect place and that everyone had his best interest at heart and that was a far cry from the reality on the ground.

The presence of a dream is the presence of dream killers. Dream killers emerge when you start dreaming. When you stop dreaming, they stop bothering you. When you abandon the dream, they abandon you. You do not even need to begin working on your dream and your dream killers will show up. Persons who abandon their dreams abandon a fulfilled, prosperous and successful life. So if you are thinking about abandoning your dream due to the opposition you face, know that you are throwing out the baby with the bath water.

Introducing the Dream Killer – Their Mission

Joseph's brothers spelt out the ultimate mission of dream killers in Genesis 37:20,

"Come therefore, let us now kill him and cast him into some

pit; and we shall say, 'Some wild beast has devoured him.' We shall see what will become of his dreams!"

Their mission is to ensure nothing becomes of your God-given dream. Their mission is to ensure your dream does not bear fruit. As long as you do nothing about the dream, they have succeeded. When they fail at this, they will work to stagnate the progress of your dream. They will suppress it.

Some dream killers will go to every extent necessary to ensure they achieve this mission. This group will kill the dreamer, if need be, to ensure nothing becomes of the dream. Some of Joseph's brothers agreed to kill him to ensure his dreams were not fulfilled. That is how far some dream killers will go just because of your dream. Jesus said in John 10:10 that,

"The thief does not come except to steal, and to kill, and to destroy. I have come that they may have life, and that they may have it abundantly."

The dream killer will steal the dream, kill and destroy it if given the opportunity. As their name goes, so are they; they are dream killers. They come to kill your dream.

Do you know that even God has an enemy to His dreams? Satan and his cohorts along with the sinful nature of man are his arch-enemies. They are no match for him; they are not in God's class though God has allowed them to have some power – limited though they are, they use it to oppose His plans and works. If there are dream killers against the dreams of God, what makes you think you do not have or will not have dream killers around you? One of the best ways to deal with dream killers is to expect them. When you accept their existence, you expect them and therefore prepare for them.

Introducing Dream Killers – Their Different Forms

Dream killers come in different shades and forms. They come in the form of spiritual forces, people, situations and even institutions which endanger the life of the dream and the dreamer.

The arch dream killer is satan and his demonic forces. Amongst the things he steals, kills and destroys include God-given dreams. Satan loves to turn dreams from God into a nightmare. Any good thing God has for you, the devil does not want you to have it. When God wants to give you something, he wants to prevent you from having it. He works ceaselessly to ensure the dream does not come to pass.

Dream killers also come in the form of people. There are people who are not happy with the progress of others especially when this progress places them behind. They will work tooth and nail to hinder your forward movement for varied motivations. Greed, envy and jealousy are some of the motivations of such persons. Do not think everyone likes you. You are not in the good books of everyone. It is not everyone who talks with you with a smile who smiles at your dream. It is not every brother or sister who likes you.

The proximity of a person to you does not determine whether he is a dream killer or a dream enabler. In other words, dream killers can be as close as a family member and as distant from you as someone you don't even know exists. Joseph's own brothers were his dream killers. One of Jesus' disciples was a dream killer. When Joseph was sold by his brothers and worked as a slave in Potiphar's house, his master's wife became a dream killer. Dream killers are found everywhere.

Another dream killer is situations or conditions. A particular condition, state of affairs or circumstances - be it spiritual, physical, mental or environmental can be designed to work against your dream. For instance, sin, poverty, sickness, conflict, the absence of technology and ignorance can kill your dream. The most powerful condition of man that works against his dreams is the condition of sin - our sinful nature. Sin (missing the mark) is what threw overboard all the good thoughts God had for man in the Garden of Eden. Every adverse condition we find ourselves in is a product of sin. The sinful nature has worked against man, making us live a life that is far less than God's best for us. We have also aggravated this situation by further creating other conditions that kill dreams.

Institutions can also work against a dream. When an institution works against a dream, the strength of the institution determines the impact of its actions against the dream. When God called Moses to lead the Israelites out of slavery in Egypt to the Promised Land, it was a dream He was giving him. But that dream required him to fight against the most powerful king on earth at that time – Pharaoh. Pharaoh was not just a person, he was an institution. Martin Luther King had the FBI of the United States working against his fight for equality for African-Americans. There are times when an institution may not officially work against a dream but a person in a position of power may be using his influence against you.

The Most Dangerous Dream Killer

Dream killers are usually thought of as external people and situations that work against our God-given dream. We usually attribute the opposition we face in pursuit of our dreams to the work of satan, a person or a certain group of people. At the mention of 'dream killers', our brain is wired to think of that person out there. This perception is common amongst Africans; we have a fixation towards persons actively working against our progress. By including this chapter on dream killers in this book, it means I agree with the proposition that there are other persons (be it human beings or evil spirits) who work against the achievement of our dreams. What I do not agree with however, is the extremist approach whereby every challenge you face in the pursuit of your dream is as a result of an external threat.

The dream killer is not always the other person; it could be you. Apart from God, the most important factor in the fulfillment of your dreams is YOU. It is not your government, your parents, your employer, a friend or some other person or institution. It is YOU. As the most important determiner in the fulfillment of your dream, you can also be the most dangerous threat to it. God may have a dream for you but self-sabotage destroys your ability to fulfill the dream. You may be the most dangerous threat to yourself and dream. Self-sabotage is the most dangerous sabotage.

In Joshua 1:8, Joshua is made aware of this principle of life:

*"This Book of the Law shall not depart from **your** mouth, but **you** shall meditate in it day and night, that **you** may observe to do according to all that is written in it. For then **you** will make **your** way prosperous, and then **you** will make good success."*

God desired prosperity and good success for Joshua. His experience of God's dream for him was dependent on what He did with the word of God. God used the pronouns 'you' and 'your' six times in this single verse revealing the role he played in ensuring the dream is achieved. Every dream from God is a partnership between God and us.

He has a part to play and we also have a part to play. Do you notice that satan is not here in the picture at all. As long as Joshua does what God instructs him to do, he keeps satan out of his dream. His success was therefore not influenced by what God desires for him or what God will do for Him but by what he also does.

Jonah's life buttresses this truth. God gave him an assignment which he should have added to his dreams for life. The opposite was however the case - he refused to accept the responsibility to pursue it. The greatest opposition to his assignment was him. The Israelites who left Egypt for the Promised Land were also their own saboteurs. God's dream for them was to get them to the Promised Land but their mindset, behavior and confession killed the dream.

Life Lessons from Two Prostitutes

There is an interesting account in 1 Kings Chapter 3;

"Then came there two women who were harlots, unto the King, and stood before hm. And the one woman said, "O my lord, I and this woman dwell in one house; and I was delivered of a child with her in the same house. And it came to pass the third day after that I was delivered, that this woman was delivered also: and we were together; there was no stranger with us in the house, save we two in the house. And this woman's child died in the night; because she overlaid it.

And she arose at midnight, and took my son from beside me, while thine handmaid slept, and laid it in her bosom, and laid her dead child in my bosom. And when I rose in the morning to give my child suck, behold it was dead: but when I had considered it in the morning, behold, it was not my son, which I did bear." 1 Kings 3:16-21 KJV.

A woman gave birth and three days after, she accidentally lay on her baby, killing him in the process. She conceived the child for nine months but killed him in minutes. It is obvious she did not deliberately sleep on the baby but she should have been more careful and vigilant. Today, we do not hear such stories but there are people who conceive and birth a dream but end up killing the dream through carelessness and lack of vigilance. A moment of carelessness can lead to the collapse of something you have taken years to conceive, birth and nurture. May every spirit of carelessness be kept far from you in Jesus name.

Now let's talk about the other woman in this picture whose baby was stolen by the other who lay on hers. She could have kept good watch over her baby whilst she slept. She never assumed any danger happening to her baby once she was with her colleague under the same roof. In the midnight whilst she slept, her baby was taken away. I have an advice for you. Be careful how you sleep! There may be thieves right under your roof who are looking for something precious in your possession. Pray that negligence or lack of vigilance would be far away from your courts. Love your dream, protect your dream and be watchful as dream stealers are also dream killers. Be careful who you share your dreams with - business ideas, creative concepts, music, art and poetry when shared can be stolen and produced by others who did not conceive the dream.

Different Levels, Different Dream Killers

As I stated earlier, whenever there is a dream, they will also be dream killers. As long as we are alive, we must have dreams so dream killers will also continue to be with us. But I have noticed that apart from their 'omnipresence' in our lives, they increase their operations against us as we also advance in the pursuit of our dreams. In other words, the higher we climb on our dream ladder, the greater the fight becomes.

A study of Joseph's life reveals that he had dream killers at every stage before he saw the achievement of his dream. When he was in his father's house, his dream killers were his brothers. Before then, though his brothers hated him, he was the beloved son of his father who was a rich man. He had enemies but his life condition was not as it became when he arrived in Egypt. In Egypt, his life condition deteriorated further as he became a slave. In Potiphar's house, he knew his flesh could also work against him so he fled from the temptation. This worsened his life condition further as he was framed and thrown into jail. His life condition had deteriorated to the lowest ebb – a prisoner.

In my geography class, I was told that "the higher you go in the atmosphere, the cooler it becomes". In life, the higher you climb, the hotter it becomes but if you have gone through the mill, you are able to handle every difficult situation successfully. Some preachers have carved the statement, "new levels new devils".

How to Deal With Dream Killers

Understand that Some Dream Killers are Your Dream Enablers

The intention and actions of dream killers are to steal, kill and destroy the dream and the dreamer. But I have noticed that God permits some dream killers to be around for a purpose. Since the fall of man, dream killers have always been around and God permits some of them to lurk around in our lives.

God does this because He is able to turn dream killers into dream enablers. He allows them to back-bite us so that we can move forward in life. These are the enemies who God will only prepare a table for you when they are present in your life. Once again, the life of Joseph is an example. In Genesis 45:5 and 8, he told his brothers:

"But now, do not therefore be grieved or angry with yourselves because you sold me here; for God did sent me before you to preserve life.

So now it was not you who sent me here, but God; and He has made me a father to Pharaoh, and the lord of all his house, and a ruler throughout all the land of Egypt."

We describe his brothers as dream killers but here, Joseph is pointing out that they were not dream killers but rather, dream enablers. God used them to send him to Egypt to preserve life. If God used Joseph's brothers to move him towards his destiny, then dream killers are at times necessities on the journey to fulfilling the dream. You need them to realize a lot of things about God and yourself.

The actions of every dream killer in your life can be converted into forward movement towards your dream. God can turn the actions of the people who hate you into accelerators to move you towards the fulfillment of your dream. How He will do it in your life, I do not know but He has proven over the years that He is an expert in that. Do not try to comprehend how He will do it because you may not be able to.

In addition, God permits dream killers to mature us through tests of our faith. Tests and trials are a vital part of the Christian journey. They are inevitable in our walk with God. They come to prove how committed you are to the dream and your level of faith you have in the God who gave you the dream. According to Apostle James,

"...count it all joy when you fall into various trials, knowing that the testing of your faith produces patience. But let patience have its perfect work, that you may be perfect and complete, lacking nothing." James 1:2-4

The purpose of trials is to make us perfect and complete; to mature us. There is a certain level in the fulfillment of your dream that requires a lot of maturity to get there. The higher you want to go in the fulfillment of your dream, the more mature you must be. It follows then that the more trials God allows you go through, the more you are becoming ready to fulfill His purpose for your life.

If your life is full of trials today, then expect God to do something great through you tomorrow - something beyond your wildest dreams.

Simply Endure

Since God permits some dream killers to be in your life, you just have to endure them because God will not take them out of your life. They need to be present for the dream to be fulfilled. Prayer does not take such persons away. I am not saying though that every dream killer should be tolerated. Jesus endured the persecutions of His own people because it was a significant part of accomplishing his mission on earth. Most Christians today are not willing to endure opposition on their way to achieving their dreams and subsequently abandon it on the way.

Shut Your Mouth and Shut Them Out

Though God used Joseph's brothers to push him forward, if he had not told them about his dream, their hatred for him would not have worsened. He was simply naïve. When you get to know who your dream killers are, you do not have to share your dream with them. Be careful who you share your dreams with.

Apart from shutting your mouth, you may also have to shut them out of your life. The people you allow into your life are either dream killers or dream enablers. Dream killers are to be shut out of your life. You should not operate an open door policy for everyone. Access into your life should be restricted to people you can trust to be on your side. When you open your life's dreams to everyone, you may be shutting some doors unknowingly, so be discreet.

The Power of Personal Fellowship with God

Fellowship with God is possibly the most powerful way of dealing with your dream killers. By fellowship, I am referring to a personal consistent life of prayer, Bible study and fasting. Through fellowship, we receive spiritual strength to endure the dream killers who God permits to lurk around our lives. We may not always know who these dream killers are but God knows them and so supplies us with the strength to endure their presence. Through fellowship, we receive inner guidance about dream killers we should dissociate from. Fellowship enables our spiritual antenna to detect signals of the dream killers we should avoid. When we pray, the barriers that dream killers mount before us are brought down; traps they have set up for us are destroyed.

My prayer for you is that the actions of every dream killer around you will become a propeller for the fulfillment of your dream. May every evil intention be turned into good for you. May you receive the strength of an ox to endure the dream killers God permits into your life.

I terminate the assignment of every dream killer in your life.

CHAPTER 14

I HAVE A DREAM...

WHEN ALL ELSE FAILS, STRIVE TO KEEP YOUR DREAM.

I have a dream that one day **African countries** will:

Not be found in the basket of Third World countries but will be on the showroom of First World nations.

- Emerge from the ruins of under-development and join the league of super powers.

- Be an oasis of peace and stability and not a den of conflicts.

- No longer be referred to as the cradle of civilization but the model of civilization.

- Become the breeding ground for ethical, transformational servant leaders and not selfish, corrupt leaders.

- Shift from being a continent of consumers and to become the world's factory, producing for the global marketplace.

- Become citadels of excellence and not a reference point for mediocrity.

- Be the desire of all nations and they will flock to behold the wonders of our development.

- Lend to many nations instead of globe-trotting for support

- Become the center for training world class scientists, entrepreneurs, engineers, leaders, athletes to mention a few.

We have a dream and we will dream big even in our small places.

I Have A Dream That One Day...

- The **Holy Spirit** (The Third Person Of The Trinity) will become the most important person on earth.

- The knowledge of the Holy Spirit as the unseen agent of God on planet earth will transcend all knowledge.

- Through the power of the Holy Spirit, revivals will be sparked, heaven will be populated and hell de-populated; that there will be an avalanche of healings and miracles; deep hurts will be healed and bondages will be broken.

- The power of the Holy Spirit shall overcome all forms of satanic powers. Addictions and spells will be broken and psychic powers and voodoo powers will not stand the believer.

- Through the wisdom of the Holy Spirit, great ideas will be birthed, complex problems will be solved, great inventions will be created and solutions to the problems of mankind will be born.

- The Holy Spirit will show himself strong on behalf of the people of God.

I Have A Dream That One Day...

The **Word Of God** (The Bible) will be ...

- The most significant book on the planet and will not be pushed to the background.

- Found in every home, school and office.

- The most important textbook for educating children and the manual for life.

- The all time best-seller, the most read and applied book in every nation.

- The most sought after book in the world with people travelling far and near to listen to the wisdom from it.

- The ultimate source of wisdom and counsel for solving

the deteriorating problems facing mankind.

- The knowledge of the Lord will fill the whole earth through the Word of God.

I Have A Dream That One Day...

The Church (the called-out ones) will be...

- The most influential organization on the earth, exalted and established as a model for and above all other organizations.

- The church will not be relegated into the museums of history but will be relevant in every community; all church buildings that have been deserted will be restored.

- The church will be the place where all nations will flock for solutions to their problems and answers to questions as she dispenses the manifold wisdom of God.

- The kings of the earth shall flock to the church after seeing the brightness of her rising.

- The church will be the refuge and the place for transforming the unsaved, unrighteous, the ignorant, the sick, the poor, the broken hearted and the depressed.

- The church will become a formible force, destroying all gates of hades.

- The church will be a financial powerhouse; the abundance of the seas and the treasures of secret places shall be her portion; she shall lend to many and borrow from none.

- The church will be the rebuilder of ghettos, slums and abandoned projects, restoring them to a glory never seen before on this earth.

- I have a dream of a glorious church, without spot, blemish or wrinkle.

I HAVE A DREAM

evangsal

POWER 4 TODAY
117 BRUCE GROVE
TOTTENHAM
London. N17 6UR
United Kingdom

Tel: 020 8801 4939
Email: info@bishopansah.org
Website: www.bishopansah.org

SUBSCRIPTION FORM

For your copy of this and forth coming quarterlies of this devotional, kindly fill out the form below.

Name:

Tel. No:

Email:

Residential Address:

Post Code

RECOMMEND A FRIEND

Please fill out this form and we will happily contact the recipient.

Tel. No:

Email:

Residential Address:

Post Code:

www.ingramcontent.com/pod-product-compliance
Lightning Source LLC
LaVergne TN
LVHW022341080426
835508LV00012BA/1294